BLOOMING *Into*
THE PROMISE

How I, A Latina, Broke My Generational Cycle and Manifested My Vision

ALICIA T. BASURTO

Published by Victorious You Press™ Charlotte NC, USA

TITLE: BLOOMING INTO THE PROMISE
First Printed: 2024
Cover Designer: Nadia Monsano – Elite Creations
Editor: Leslie Cottrell
ISBN: 978-1-959719-43-4
ISBN: (Ebook) 978-1-959719-44-1
Library of Congress Control Number: 2024921426

Printed in the United States of America

For details email joan@victoriousyoupress.com

or visit us at www.victoriousyoupress.com

ACKNOWLEDGMENTS

I want to express my deepest gratitude to my family for their unwavering support throughout this journey. To my spouse, Manuel Basurto, who endured late nights and countless revisions with a smile. To my children, Emmanuel Basurto, Stephanie Contreras, and Jordan Basurto, who accepted the challenge to help and inspire me with boundless imagination. Lastly, to my parents, who did the best they knew.

CONTENTS

Foreword   1

1. The Big Day   4

2. The Magical Moment   10

3. A Dreamer With A Vision   20

4. Accomplishing Goals   34

5. New Opportunities   42

6. Determined To Rise   58

7. My Why   72

8. Fulfilling Dreams   88

9. True Champion   96

10. Mercedes Benz   102

11. Hitting My Stride   112

12. Overcoming Difficulties   120

13. Bittersweet   128

14. Internal Fire   136

15. Working Smarter, Not Harder   152

16. Evolving World   158

17. God Is Good   166

Sources   171

Alicia T. Basurto   174

FOREWORD

In the vibrant tapestry of immigrant narratives, some stories radiate with extraordinary resilience and determination. Alicia "Alice" Tenorio Basurto's journey is one such luminous thread—a testament to the unyielding strength of the human spirit.

Born into a family of migrant farm workers from Guanajuato, Mexico, Alice's life unfolded amidst the strawberry fields of Oxnard, California, a landscape shaped by sacrifice and hope for a brighter future.

Alice's story transcends the ordinary. Despite facing adversity and enduring hurtful slurs, she refused to surrender to the limitations imposed upon her. Instead, she forged ahead with steadfast determination, carving her path and defying the odds.

Our lives intersected over three decades ago, and it has been my absolute honor to witness Alice's remarkable journey firsthand. Together, we have shared countless memories, both professional and personal, alongside our families.

Through the highs and lows of life, we have stood by each other's side—celebrating milestones, offering unwavering support, and cherishing the bonds of camaraderie forged in the crucible of shared experiences.

It has been a privilege to preside over some of Alice's banquets, commemorating her achievements and the indelible mark she has left on countless lives. And now, to pen the foreword of her book is a testament to the enduring impact of her story.

As we embark on this journey through the pages of Alice's life, may her story serve as a beacon of hope, inspiration, and possibility—a reminder of the transformative power of resilience, determination, and unwavering faith in the promise of tomorrow.

Jorge N. DeLeon, President

Century 21 Real Estate Alliance

Chapter One

THE BIG DAY

Every insurance salesperson dreams of selling their product and receiving an invitation to the Topper Club as a top producer. My excitement was overwhelming when I got my first invitation to the Topper Club 2004 Members Convention. The event took place in Whistler, Canada. Only in my dreams could I have traveled this far. I was born into a low-income immigrant family. Growing up, we had limited exposure to travel and none to resorts. The only countries I journeyed to, were Mexico and the United States. Never did I imagine being this far from home.

The day was here! I traveled from Los Angeles Airport to Vancouver, Canada. As we were landing, I peered through the airplane window. I saw forestry I had never seen before. Upon getting off the plane, I noticed my multi-ethnic insurance colleagues. They wore their insurance attire with company emblems, traveling from all over the country. A tour guide with a giant smile held our business sign, ready to take us to the resort. As I drew closer to the crowd of agents, my approach sparked conversation among them. I learned where many were from as we reciprocated congratulatory remarks. I felt in awe; a cloud of inspiration hovered over my head. I felt like I was floating. It felt gratifying to be around successful peers who also met the criteria to be invited. At that moment, I knew I had made it. My perception of my self-worth changed. I felt the shadow of my past drifting away. The facade of an agency owner's infrastructure formerly hid the boundless work ethic that I had.

A high-end, deluxe black bus driver picked us up at the airport entrance. He drove us up to the mountains of Whistler, where an extravagant resort awaited us. Again, I was shocked. I had never experienced such a trip. My humble family could never afford such a lifestyle. Finally, we reached the resort, nestled amongst the vast greenery. Entering the chilly hotel, the concierge greeted us and brought our belongings to our suite. The air was crisp inside, just as it had been outside. When we registered, the staff provided an itinerary outlining trip expectations and workshops. As a welcome, they offered us an open bar and snacks. Once we settled in, we were ready to enjoy ourselves. The first event on our itinerary was a welcome night, and everyone was invited.

The company executives congratulated us on our production and shared what to expect. I had no idea what was coming!

The next day was ceremony day. I styled my hair, applied natural makeup, and wore a sparkly, dark blue gown with black heels. My husband wore a navy suit coupled with a dark blue checkered tie. We sat at a table assigned to us in front of the stage, next to company executives dressed in luxury tuxedos and bow ties. They had a commanding presence. The awards dinner started with a fantastic cocktail hour. Our luxurious meal was filet mignon, red wine, and an exquisite cheesecake. Everything was elegantly decorated.

Announcements began for awards for agents who had performed well. Out of the blue, they announced a new award category, *Rookie Agent of the Year*, and called out my name! This latest award was for high sales production in Auto, Home, Life, Commercial, and Financial Services. My production exceeded the others. I had no idea I had done so well. I accomplished it all within my first full year as an entrepreneur. Also, I was the first Latina woman to attain such a high-level award. I started to tremble as I saw my peers stand up to applaud my support. My heart fluttered, and I felt like a movie star. At that moment, I truly believed anyone could achieve the unthinkable with hard work and dedication. If you set your mind to do what's good for others,

God will be there to bless your family every step of the way. Be sure to remain grateful and humble, and do what's good for others before your benefit with every transaction.

Chapter Two

THE MAGICAL MOMENT

In 1962, I was born to a family of 10 (four boys and six girls) in the small town of Moroleón, Guanajuato, Mexico. Moroleón is in central Mexico, 200 miles from Mexico City. The town was founded in 1929 and had a population of 12,000 people. It was considered an essential shopping destination for clothes in Guanajuato. Clothing stores lined the streets for miles and was one of the leading cities in Mexico's textile industry.

Our family had many prejudices. My father, Jesus, was a rigorous man and imposed strict rules and guidelines on our family. He was a very responsible, disciplined, traditional, and hard-working man. He was relatively tall at 5'11 and had a medium build, light complexion, and green hazel eyes. My mother, Trini, was a humble, spiritual, loving, hard-working woman, always praying for our family. She was only 5 feet tall and had a robust build, olive skin, and brown eyes. My parents were married in August 1946. They had been married for 64 years when Mom passed away in 2010. My father was a professional weaver (trabajo de telar) specializing in Mexican Rebozos (Shawls).

Dad heard of an opportunity to apply for work in the United States, or "El Norte" as it was called for us. This was a type of lottery; if he got lucky, he would get hired. After he applied, he received a notification of his approval a few months later. He followed every requirement, from a physical to a background check, and passed them all. Trying to be a better provider for our family, he joyfully told everyone, "I accepted the opportunity. I am thrilled to become a bracero." The program was from 1942 to 1964. The agreement permitted Mexicans to work in the US temporarily for agricultural purposes. It was created to fill labor shortages in the United States during World War II (Liaga-Linares, L).

My father had to sacrifice a lot for us. Jesus didn't mind the strenuous labor in tough conditions. His goal was to lift us out of poverty to a brighter future. Dad did a fantastic job; he was very proud to accept this new challenge and did everything he could to provide for us. He had terrible stories of picking cotton in Arizona's scorching weather and living in cramped men's camp quarters.

My dad chose to remain in the United States and comply with all orders until we could join him legally. He was against illegal entry into the United States. He would not betray the country that allowed him to work toward a better future. After a few years passed and he had proven himself, he could apply for permanent residency. He was overjoyed and proud to be able to bring his family to the United States legally.

Dad found excellent work opportunities in Oxnard, California. He knew the weather would allow long-term opportunities for work. He worked as a checker at Coastal Growers Lemon Association in Oxnard. In 1960, Oxnard was a quaint beach town with a population of around 45,000, but that population grew exponentially because of agriculture.

First, he applied to take my oldest brother, Jesus, with him and then my mom Trini. After them came my older sisters, Imelda and Carmen. Everyone, including my mom, started working in agriculture as soon as they arrived. From tomatoes and chiles to lemons and strawberries, depending on the season. Despite their inexperience, they refused to give up on this type of work.

I immigrated with my other five siblings, Rosa, Roberto, Delfino, Lula, and Victor, in 1970. My sister Teresa never came to the U.S. My older siblings and my mom were already working by this time. What affected me was that my parents did not believe in getting financial help. Their solid ethical values reminded me of the importance of working hard for one's goals. My parents taught us to avoid exploiting the government and to work hard for our income.

We had to meet various requirements and complete extensive paperwork to secure a green card. My parents had a good family friend who had his gas expenses paid. He would drive us to Mexico City (five hours away) for all the paperwork and various appointments. I remember seeing the road through a hole in the car floor. I was terrified, but it was their only affordable transportation.

I arrived in the United States of America by bus. I remember being extremely excited when we crossed the border. The roads and freeways were wide and clean. It was more expansive than the roads in Mexico. Everything seemed so beautiful and enchanted, it was startling! Sitting with my siblings on that big bus, I daydreamed about our new home in the United States.

I was a shy, and insecure 7-year-old girl. Once we settled into our new home, we got beautiful clothes from the thrift store. Mom was so excited to bring these clothes home for us.

I remember my favorite was a lovely pink dress that I fell in love with. Mom said I wanted to wear it every day and didn't mind at all that it was used.

I had only gone to kindergarten in Mexico. I was so excited to go to school that I got my uniform ready the night before. I had trouble sleeping since I wanted to start but knew I would be behind the other children. Things had already changed drastically. We were starting school in another country and finally had a permanent house. It was a yellow, one-story old home in an industrial area that had a big yard to play in. We all had mixed emotions since we only spoke Spanish. The schools were solely English-speaking. I went to Driffill Elementary School with my two older brothers, who were 9 and 11. We felt petrified and cried when we had to leave one another to go to our classrooms. We didn't speak any English, so the school authorities transferred us to McKinna Elementary School after just a few weeks. The school district was nice enough to provide a tutor, a lovely lady named Ms. Saucedo. She was perhaps a second-generation Latina woman, as her English and Spanish were fluent. She had just a small group of students and was very helpful and kind. We quickly learned the alphabet and words like apple, chair, table, etc. She made it fun. I loved her.

Because we were learning so well, Ms. Saucedo invited us to go skating as a special treat. I could not skate at all! Growing up, I never experienced many sports. I felt scared and kept falling. She had so much patience. She never gave up on me and eventually, I became an avid skater. I felt so proud of myself. The promise of more skating trips motivated us to do our homework and polish our speech and pronunciation. Learning English was difficult. I realized it was an early lesson that anything worthwhile, takes work. I saw Ms. Saucedo as our angel who welcomed us to America. Despite my parents' general mistrust, she earned their favor by visiting us in our home.

Mom signed me up for catechism. I learned how to pray and did my first communion. On Mother's Day, when I was eight, we celebrated both events in Moroleón, Guanajuato. I got to wear my long dress and a beautiful crown. The church smelled like gorgeous fresh flowers — a gift to my mom on her special day. We had a Mexican breakfast of bread and delicious hot chocolate at my Madrina's home. After the celebration, my faith in God got more robust. Every night, I prayed to the angels and God for guidance, strength, and knowledge. I felt he heard me, and I began to feel like I was born under a star. If I had my mind set on something, I knew God would make it happen. As I got older, my faith grew even stronger. Mom was pleased I knew how to pray. She always said if I didn't follow God's wisdom and guidance, he would punish me, and I believed her. It built my ethical character, and a clear conscience was very important to me. Every Sunday, Mom would make us go with her to Our Lady of Guadalupe in Oxnard. She claimed that laziness was caused by the devil. We didn't want that, so we were happy to attend church. I saw how humble she was and always prayed for a peaceful life for us and everyone. It affected my life because she told me never to fight, but to talk things through. She taught me to learn to communicate and be diplomatic. "Remember, your dad is against fighting, especially in school," she would remind us. Violence in our lives was not acceptable. Our parents prohibited us from using "bad words" or straightforward negative language. Our home was always quiet. Dad could be tired or moody, so we'd rather not say a word. At times, we feared him.

Dad insisted on us completing our chores perfectly, or he would make us redo them. We knew that laziness was not allowed in our house. Mom warned, "Your father won't appreciate 'this' or 'that.'" Now, I see how much that toughness helped us. It shaped all of us to be responsible and well-disciplined. My siblings are all very responsible. My father made sure my mom taught us girls how to cook at a very early age. We also helped her with the dishes every day. According to him, girls belonged in the kitchen. The boys worked outside the home; everything from landscaping to car mechanics. We all turned out to be good people.

Chapter Three

A DREAMER WITH A VISION

While I was in elementary school, I felt grateful to be getting an American education. I followed all the rules and learned fast to earn awards! My favorite award was Student of the Month. I received that recognition a few months prior. I felt sad because my parents could not attend assemblies to share in my joy. They were always working and could not ask for permission to miss work since it was agriculture. They were not allowed to take time off and were not involved with our education.

My fifth-grade teacher at Sierra Linda School in Oxnard taught us about Japan's culture. We learned about everything from origami art to rice candies and paper lamps. I admired their rich culture. I told myself, "One day, I will have a wonderful career, save money, and travel." When I would tell my mom about my dreams, she'd ask me to stop saying unrealistic things. She said that our family was on a different path.

My sixth-grade teacher's preference was art projects. He taught us about paper mâché. For one of our projects, I made a giraffe. Even though I worked on it fast, it came out beautifully and I won the contest. I always hurried because I wanted to be recognized and stand out. He suggested I pursue art given my talent and potential. Hearing that comment made my day. I was not used to hearing positivity at home, so I focused on positivity at school. I began training my mind to be positive and trust God. I never wasted time; my goal was to impress teachers. Even though I was only 12 years old, I saw the value of education, and it was my comfort zone. I didn't care if I was "the teacher's pet," as they'd call it. I just knew I could learn more from the teachers than anyone else.

When I finished grade school, it was time to move on to Fremont Junior High. I was still shy and insecure as a teenager and struggled with self-esteem issues. On Mondays, the girls would ask what I did over the weekend. Typically, my mom and dad had us hang out with them. I felt embarrassed and different from the other girls. They'd go to parties, movies, and concerts. I'd tell them we went shopping and ended the conversation. Usually, we'd go to church,

McDonald's for lunch, and then the swap meet. Occasionally, we'd go to the park for a picnic as a family. We couldn't go anywhere alone. I believed everyone looked at me as a thirteen-year-old who still hung out with her parents. So, instead, I'd focus on my grades and only had a few friends. School was my only distraction away from my parents, so I took advantage and tried to enjoy it.

At age 14, when I was promoted from Junior High, Dad refused to let me go to graduation night. I was despondent. He thought it was dangerous for his daughter to be out at night. Instead, we stayed home. Yes, we were overprotected, but there was nothing we could do. Mom had to follow his orders so she couldn't speak up on our behalf. We were used to it. But deep inside, I had hopes and dreams. Let me tell you, never allow your environment to crush your beliefs and goals.

If I stayed in school, my dad assumed I was going to have a boyfriend. So, instead, he preferred I work in agriculture just as he and my mom did. In his mind, 14 was old enough to hold a job. Looking back now, at 14, you are still just a teenager trying to fit in. It's too early for such a big responsibility. When he heard a coworker needed a babysitter, he decided that would be my job. I would have to drop out of school. Mom was sad but had to agree. She talked about the relevance of school when my husband would just prevent me from working after we married. She felt it was important that we did what our dad said. For a year, I took care of sweet little Chato, who was just one year old. That year, I became depressed and would cry myself to sleep. I didn't want to cause problems for my mom and dad, so I complied. This was not a happy time for me. After a year, someone notified the school district in Oxnard that I was no longer attending school. They came to our home looking for me! They pressured my dad, and he had to agree to let me attend High School. Despite feeling happy, I also felt embarrassed and unmotivated. After all, I had lost an entire year! It wasn't easy catching back up again. I struggled and my grades went down. Sadly, I didn't care. I started focusing more on looking for part-time jobs after school by searching the high school bulletin boards. This brought me some excitement. I felt I'd get hired quickly because of my great attitude in job interviews. I learned I would get hired by showing interest and being 100% willing to learn. This plan had no space for negativity. I felt blessed to be able to look for work.

When I was 15, my mom took me to work picking strawberries in the summer. This job involved being assigned a line, with each person getting their own row. You got a wire box for the strawberries. You had to stay in a hunched-over position for speed's sake. After a few shifts, your hands would turn black, and the discoloration would remain on your hands for weeks. I have a somber image embedded in my brain of my mother on all fours, picking strawberries. She found it challenging to maintain a crouched position for long periods. I still think about it to this day. Lunchtime maintained our sanity. When the catering truck arrived at lunch break to sell chili relleno burritos, we knew they would be terrific. Agriculture is such physically hard work. Even looking forward to lunch was a relief.

After the strawberry season ended, my older sister bought a 1977 Chevy Camaro with her savings. Dad insisted I go with her to find work. He didn't want her going alone. We headed for Colonia (a Spanish-speaking community) in Oxnard. Contractors would gather there every morning to hire people as day workers. Mostly men came there looking for day jobs, but we didn't care. We just wanted to work. My sister had a car payment now. Since she couldn't be alone, I had no choice but to support her by going along.

We eagerly responded when contractors asked for additional workers. As girls, we got hired quickly, usually to pick chilies. It rained one day, and I recall us wearing plastic boots that went over our regular street shoes. They became cumbersome, and we had to shuffle around with the bags of chilies. My sister laughed as she tried to keep me motivated. I was mad. Deep inside, I thought I could do something better since I spoke English and most of the other workers didn't. It was backbreaking work; we had to carry big trash cans full of chilies and take them to a trailer, which got emptied.

After the season ended, I moved on. Soon I found a new job as a seamstress at a small Puerto Rican-owned factory. It was near our home so my sister could drive me there. I was going to be trained to sew on a sewing machine. I remember learning on the first attempt with the overlock machine. My boss liked the fact I was learning so fast. I ended up loving this work. We used to sew charming little tennis uniforms.

An opportunity with more hours at McDonald's opened. I insisted to my mom that I wanted to work there. She was certain that my dad would refuse because of my separation from the family. Somehow, she convinced him and agreed. I went straight to the interview and got hired immediately. I was so happy! First, they trained me on the register, and I learned all about customer service. Cross-selling cherry and apple pies, drinks, and fries came easily to me. God began planting a seed for my future in this job without me even knowing it. Who knew that sales training would be part of my future insurance career? I enjoyed learning so much that the store implemented a contest during the lunch break. It was called "The Speeder of the Month." I took this seriously and won two months in a row for taking the most orders during the lunch rush. That "Speeder of the Month" contest made me so happy. I discovered more and more how much I loved competitions. My hustling, discipline, and responsibility caught the management's attention. Soon, they offered me the position of crew leader. My mom said I could not work nights, though. I loved my job, and I loved being out of agricultural work. Working at McDonald's made me feel important. I had the privilege of working inside, not out in the sun. We had air conditioning and heat! I felt so proud.

Unfortunately, when I turned 18, my parents retired and moved back to Moroleón, Guanajuato, Mexico. My four siblings who were still single and living at home, had no choice but to go along. In Mexican culture, kids don't move out until they are married. None of us were certain about relocating to Mexico. As soon as we arrived, I got a job at a clothing store. I was always lucky getting hired, but especially so having just come from the USA. I was presentable and bilingual, so I stood out. A few months later, I told my dad I wanted to return to school. I had never graduated since I got behind that year I had missed. Dad refused. He said I would probably follow in my sister's footsteps by getting married, quitting my job, and returning to the USA to work in agriculture. I did not give up and kept insisting I go back to school. Eventually, I wore him down, and he agreed. I offered to work part-time to pay my tuition at Colegio Fray Miguel F. Zavala. This college was a private all-girl catholic school. I signed up to become a certified public assistant. My goal was to work as a teller at a local bank. I wanted to dress professionally, look lovely, and work in a positive office environment. I truly enjoyed the entire school year, from the girls to the ambiance. Everyone there was friendly, including the nun teachers who were always pleasant to us and accommodating. Because I spoke and wrote English so well, even better than my teacher, I was exempt from the English as a second language class. She even asked if I could help her with the class. Having that role made me feel important, which thrilled me. This began my love for Mexico's education system.

My sister and her friends invited me to join them on a walk at Jardin de Moroléon. This gathering place was a Mexican tradition. Years later, I discovered it was the same spot where my parents met. Little did I know how important that walk would be. I met the man who would become my husband that night. Manuel lived in Mexico City, a densely populated city, and the capital of Mexico. Manuel was visiting the area with friends. It was so different from his home city that he fell in love with our small town. He and his friends approached our group and started a conversation by introducing themselves. He was looking right at me, so we started to talk. It was exciting for both of us. Manuel was tall, muscular, and handsome with an intense tan. Who knew this was how we would meet? We were both 18. Because of my strict upbringing, I still felt like a young girl and was still shy and insecure. Manuel loved that about me. He had never met a girl who had been so protected by her parents. I had longed to find someone who could understand my situation. Love sparked between us instantly. I shared my grandmother's address and phone number with Manuel because my dad didn't allow me to have a boyfriend just yet. This strictness by my dad was one reason I thought I'd never meet someone who could understand my home life. Some guys had an interest in me in high school, but they backed off once they discovered my restrictions. I twisted this all around and thought I was just weird and ugly. I appreciated that this new guy knew what he was getting into and still wanted to see me. In fact, he seemed to understand me completely. He felt like the perfect person for me. When we knew each other better, he admitted that he immediately saw I was shy, analytical, quiet, and intelligent. Since I had never had a social life, I didn't believe any of it. Despite this, I kept seeing him whenever he could return to my town.

When we met, he had just started school and was working in a clothing store on the weekends. After we became official, he visited me every other week. He would travel about five hours on the public bus, which was easier than driving his 1972 VW Bug. We would spend a couple of hours together and he would hold my hand around the Jardin. I could not get in his car when he drove it. Only "bad girls" did that. He sacrificed a lot to make our relationship work. Coming to see me so often was not easy on him. Manuel was busy working at the Universidad Autonoma de Mexico and attending college part-time to become an attorney. He would leave for home at midnight on Sunday and go to work at 6 a.m. Manuel would sleep on the bus ride back to be ready for work in the morning. After about a year and a half, Manuel proposed to me, and I was thrilled to accept. However, my father adamantly opposed our marriage. Dad refused to agree because he didn't like the idea of me marrying an outsider. After some time, I gained my mom's support. It wasn't easy, but after hearing that I would elope if she disapproved, she finally softened. I knew I would never do that, but I needed my parents' blessing-or at least my mother's. After Mom agreed to support us, Manuel drove us and his sister to look for a dress. He was so happy that he could buy my dress out of his savings. The dress was 10,000 pesos or $300 US dollars. My dad stayed true to his word and refused to attend our wedding. Not having his blessing made me feel so sad. I knew I had to get past it and not allow it to bother me. I was so in love that nothing could interfere with this happiness.

Our wedding day was February 19th, in my hometown of Moroléon. The wedding mass was at Templo del Senor de Esquipulitas, but the reception was 5 hours away in Mexico City. My mother-in-law, Lupe took over planning the reception, and I let her do it. In fact, I was grateful she volunteered. The reception was unique! We had the reception party on the first floor of their narrow three-story home. It wasn't what I had envisioned, but I really didn't care. I knew I was marrying the love of my life. My mother-in-law prepared the traditional Mexican meal, of delicious turkey mole with rice and salad.

After Manuel and I married, we ended up doing just what my dad had predicted. We both quit school and moved to Mexico City. I was so in love I didn't care about leaving my family behind. My mom was sad and worried that I was moving so far away. She asked my mother-in-law to be there for me and provide support since I wouldn't know anyone. I am thankful Mom always looked out for me. We moved into my aunt-in-law's home and stayed there until July 1983. I was pregnant then, and we decided we should move to the US. We took a bus to Tijuana Baja, California. The bus was all we could afford. It was hard on me being five months pregnant to spend 30 hours on a bus. My legs swelled up, and I felt very uncomfortable. I was exhausted and felt sick. Our early days as a young married couple in the US were tough. My brother, Robert, offered us his house in Oxnard. He said we could stay there while we looked for jobs. Since I was pregnant, we decided I should stay home. After a month of job searching, my husband had not found a job. My mom called her sister, in Richmond, CA, and my cousin Lila (the sweetest lady) let us stay with her. Thank God! We were so relieved when my cousin and her husband picked us up at the Oakland airport. Finding a place to stay while pregnant was challenging. I was feeling sad and wondered if we were making the right decision. My cousin came into our lives at the perfect time.

Lila's sister Nena was married to a Chevron contractor who owned a refinery. He offered my husband a job! Manuel worked hard to show him his appreciation. Things were more challenging because my husband only spoke Spanish. Though Manuel struggled, he never gave up. He learned

English and did well in his new job. He had never done manual labor, but this job didn't scare him. We were so grateful and happy. I offered to babysit my nephew, Beto, a cute one-year-old. My cousin worked at my aunt's Mexican restaurant, Pepitos Deli and her husband was at the refinery every day. They were kind enough to give us a place to live. The least I could do was help around the house and care for the baby.

Chapter Four

ACCOMPLISHING GOALS

We were excited and oh so happy to feel welcome in our cousin's house. We had family members living in the same area where we were now, and they were very supportive. My cousin's stepdad volunteered to drive me to my doctor visits. He was a very kind, older man. He and my aunt owned a thriving Mexican restaurant, Pepito's Deli. They started the business from the bottom up and were extremely hard workers. I truly admired them.

It was Thanksgiving time, and my aunt invited us to dinner at her home. I'll never forget that day. Manuel and I walked into my aunt's house to a surprise baby shower! I thought, *What did I do to deserve all this?* We were completely taken by surprise. This party was unlike any I had experienced before. We received a shower full of gifts, including baby furniture and clothes. I couldn't believe it all, but it was such a blessing because we needed everything. We didn't have to buy clothes for our son for three years! Finally, things were looking brighter for us, and I felt covered in love and support from my family.

On November 13, 1983, our first baby was born; a son! The doctors asked Manuel if he would like to cut the umbilical cord. But after witnessing everything I went through during labor and birth, he couldn't bring himself to do it. He remained by my side through everything. It reminded me again of how blessed I was to have this man as my husband. After little Manny was born, I wanted to call my mom. I said, "Mom, the baby was born. He's healthy, cute, and looks like our side of the family!"

She replied, "Every mom believes their kids are beautiful." She wasn't used to giving or receiving compliments. That was alright; I loved her like that. I was learning little by little to look on the bright side of things.

My parents came back to Oxnard at the beginning of 1984. When we visited them, I got the urge to live closer. I suggested to Manuel that we move back to Oxnard and he agreed. It felt like my family would be complete: Mom, Dad, my husband, and our new baby boy. What else could I need? We purchased a yellow 1970 VW Bug and packed it up for the move to Oxnard. Late at night, the old car broke down in

Gaviota, CA. Little Manny was only seven weeks old. We panicked because it was freezing outside.

"Manuel, what will we do now? We forgot to buy the baby his formula!"

Manuel said, "Don't worry, we will find a way."

He saw a green truck nearby and approached to drive to ask for help.

"We're stuck on the road. We have a baby and need help! Can you help us?"

The man in the truck replied, "Certainly!" I'll give you a ride when the auto parts store opens in the morning." What a relief! He was our angel, for sure. Mom was excited for us to arrive, so I found a public phone and called her. She became distraught as I told her what had happened. Mom immediately reached out to the siblings for help. Carmen, my sister-in-law, volunteered. After a frigid night, my sister-in-law arrived. Our angel from the night before had already taken Manuel to the auto parts store. After repairing the car, we could drive home. Everything had worked out.

My husband wanted us to be happy wherever I chose for us to live. He knew I had a bond with Oxnard since I grew up there. With a great attitude, he said, "Now it's time for me to start job searching again." Without a green card (he was in the process of legal residency), it was hard for him to find work. I felt responsible for his well-being since he usually agreed to my plans to make me happy. I offered to go to work, and he could watch the baby at home. He wasn't too pleased about that idea. Since he was from the Latino culture, he didn't want to consider having his wife go to work instead of him. How could he stay home while his wife worked? He struggled to accept this idea but knew that he had no choice. Sometimes we must set our traditions aside and do what's best for the family. Despite our short time together, we prioritized our family and found common ground.

I got a job working in the strawberry fields with my mom. She helped me get a job as a checker instead of a strawberry picker. Instead of bending down to pick, this job involved standing all day. Strawberry picking is hard work—I had done it before. I respect anyone who can handle a job like that. My brother mentioned to our boss that my husband was at home babysitting. Because they needed employees, Guillermo said if my husband were a hard worker, he would hire him.

Now that we both had jobs, we knew if we continued to work hard, we could save some money. We were so full of joy. We felt motivated to become more disciplined and committed to drastically limiting our expenses. We knew it would require giving up dining out, going to the movies, and visiting expensive places. Weekends would find us going to swap meets and taking Manny to parks. We prioritized paying our rent and paying a friend for gas.

Manuel received a real career opportunity when the strawberry season ended in July. His uncle Leonel, who lived in Mexico City, offered him a job at a Mexican airline as a mechanic trainee. Unfortunately, we moved back to Mexico City, but that job offer never happened. The person who was supposed to help my husband get hired didn't show up when we went to find him. Instead, he started working at his mom's business as a delivery driver. We had saved all the money we could while working in the USA. We were eager to become homeowners. I saw an ad in the newspaper advertising townhouses for sale. We paid a down payment of $5,000 (which in present currency is worth over $15,000!) for a beautiful townhome. To our surprise, it was a scam — it was a fraudulent real estate company — and they stole our hard-earned savings. All our sacrifices were for nothing! We were inconsolable and thought, *How could this happen to us?*

My sister and her husband, living in Mexico, convinced us to move back to the States in the new year. Because of our financial woes, we agreed it was a good idea. Manuel wanted us to settle in one place and stop going back and forth. He committed to making this move work for the whole family. Once back in the US, he learned to enjoy living in another country and appreciate God's opportunities. As I look back, it was the best decision of our lives. God had a fantastic plan for us. We were desperate for a better life; we promised God and the Virgin of Guadalupe that we would get closer to them. That is a promise we have kept. We go to God and pray anytime we have adversities. With faith and doing good for others, we believe God listens. We have witnessed that he hears us many times over.

As soon as we arrived in Oxnard, we both found jobs working in the strawberry fields again. We were both so relieved to be working; we didn't care where it was. If we both had jobs, we weren't going to complain or search for the "perfect" job. We couldn't waste any more time and had to save for our future. We budgeted our money and managed our finances well enough to save and buy a $500 car. My siblings called it our "Flintstone" car because it was a square-shaped, beige 1969 Toyota Corona. Not long after we traded it for a better and more reliable car.

To make some extra money, we bought Volkswagen Beetles and flipped them. My husband, a rookie VW Mechanic, fixed them up and sold them for a profit. I would search for advertisements in the paper, and Manuel would repair them. We brought in $500 per car and made a $400 profit. We saved all that extra money.

Chapter Five

NEW OPPORTUNITIES

In June 1985, when the strawberry season was over, I could have filed for unemployment benefits. Instead, I looked for work. I bought the community newspaper like I had always done. My dad was an avid newspaper reader, and I became like him. Eventually, I found a job as a flower delivery driver. During the job interview, the interviewer hired me immediately. Manny got sick, so I had to stay home and care for him instead of starting my first day. They were unhappy with me, so I continued searching and found another job within two weeks. This was perfect timing because the car we had purchased needed car insurance. I remember helping my parents translate their insurance transactions as a teenager. Because of that, I remembered where my family's insurance agency had been located. I asked the car insurance agent about job openings as I dreamt of working in an office. He wasn't looking for help, but he told me about another agent nearby who needed someone.

He called the other agent and made an appointment for me. I immediately got excited! I was so excited, that I got to the office an hour early for the interview. The agency owner was with a client and asked why I was there so early. He glanced at the clock and sternly told me to wait instead of coming back at my appointment time. I still remember wearing a purple patterned outfit with the same color, top and bottom. That outfit made me feel like a more confident 22-year-old.

Even though I didn't graduate, I was eager to learn everything I could and give my all to a good job. My mind raced while I waited, so I spent the time practicing what to say. I was timid but confident! I said a prayer, placed myself in God's hands, and let Him take it from there. Finally, the wait was over. The owner of a top-producing insurance agency was interested in interviewing ME. How cool is that? Reading my application, he saw I had no office experience and only limited education, but a dynamic and disciplined character. My work experience was made up of labor work in the strawberry fields, McDonald's, a factory, and picking chilies.

"If I hire you, will you return to work in agriculture when the season starts again? I see they pay you more than I can afford." I assured him I was excited to work in an office and that I would not leave.

He had some conditions, including not having more children for five years or more. I accepted all the conditions, including that one. Since I would be his only employee, I understood he needed me in the office, not on maternity leave. Even though I had no previous office experience, I promised to learn everything he could teach me. He loved my dynamic, go-getter attitude. Manuel wasn't thrilled, but still supported me because he knew this was my dream job.

My new boss hired me for minimum wage and placed me on a 30-day probation. He told me other girls wanted the job, and he had plenty to choose from. Those 30 days felt like a rollercoaster. He had high expectations and kept the pressure on.

My first challenge during my probation period was his 28-year-old son, who also worked in the business. That man had his ups and downs. One day, his son removed receipts from my desk. He was off to meet a client at a house appointment after hours. I didn't know this idea wasn't allowed. How would I know? Imagine my surprise when my new boss found out, and he was upset with me. He got so angry that I lost my composure and cried. Being young and emotional, I felt hurt. I mustered the courage to say, "I didn't know I was hired to babysit your son," to my boss. That evening, my new boss's wife called to apologize for her husband's behavior. I forgave him and returned to work the next day. Perhaps someone else would have given up and resigned. I am proud that I didn't do that! My mother had taught me to always accept an apology. Learning from her example, I did the same she would have done. My mother never held a grudge, and I learned to move on like she had.

After this awkward incident, I got to know his son better. Despite occasional mood swings, he was a kind young man who excelled as an insurance expert. I learned a great deal from him. He taught me sales techniques, self-presentation, and why it was important to give 100%. He taught me to treat customers like friends and that I would see them become friends after a sale. My boss's son ended up being a big part of my training. It's important to note that I never took special classes or had specialized training. Learning happened as I went, often with the customer right in front of me. My boss's son had a special Italian suit for his big sales. His philosophy was: *Show a good professional image so people believe in you and buy your product. Practice any training you receive immediately with a customer, so you don't forget.* I took his advice precisely as he gave it, and guess what, it worked! I always had to consult my boss (his father) for non-insurance sales inquiries after that initial incident. This was a unique opportunity to establish a lifetime career. I was committed to this job to make a real financial impact on my family.

At 5 AM one morning, I received a call from our local Police Department. In just five months, I became the emergency contact for the business. I felt incredibly proud of this. I learned that someone had broken into the office and set it on fire. I asked Manuel to come with me to meet the police officers at the office. Once I got there, I called my boss to tell him the horrible news. My heart raced and tears fell down my face. How could someone do this? Thank God for insurance. We immediately set up shop in the back alley where we worked out of a mobile office. It was November during the cold and rainy season. We were all uncomfortable. It was hard for our clients to wait outside when it was raining. I didn't like the new conditions, but I also knew my boss needed me. I wouldn't quit or leave. Both my boss and his wife expressed their appreciation for my loyalty. They told me they would never forget. It was another example where I could see the direct results of my dedication and work ethic.

When we returned to the office a few months later, they trained me on selling auto and life insurance. Although I was now working in sales, my boss did not start a commission plan. I remained at an hourly rate. It never dawned on me to question this arrangement. I still felt very grateful that he had hired me. Back then, we just had a big, thick red book for auto insurance. There were no computers or fax machines. We manually computed a formula to arrive at a six-month insurance rate for each customer. I stayed focused, learned how to do it correctly, and quickly started making more sales. I felt so proud of my performance that I fell in love with the insurance profession. My boss cheered me on as he saw I was bringing in lots of new clients. He watched his business continually grow. Because of the influx of new customers, we needed more file cabinets. He also bought a brand-new Mercedes Benz and a new house. Within a few years of my arrival, his business was thriving! Our community embraced me, and I was becoming popular. I loved it—it thrilled me. I wasn't envious of his success because I believed his success was also mine. He backdated my raises about a month. It wasn't much, but at that point, I was okay with it. Selling insurance policies helped me form relationships with local realtors who recommended me to their clients. I received $35.00 for each policy. Part of my job was to drive out to inspect a new property and take Polaroid photos. My husband and kids came with me on weekends. I wasn't reimbursed for wear and tear on my car or gas. It was okay with us. Because we thought we were making extra money.

My boss had a friend who owned a vacation home. As a great producer award, he gifted me a weekend with my husband in Lake Tahoe in exchange of his friend's favorite alcohol. I invited my sister and her daughter to celebrate her 15th birthday with us.

My husband always supported me 100 percent. I'd share my daily stories of my clients with him, and he always listened. He was working nights in a cheese factory. We made things work as a team. Manuel always helped with our son. I dropped Manny off at our neighborhood babysitter, and Manuel would pick him up. I knew he'd be punctual. We were living in a mobile home in a small, modest park. Everyone there knew each other. We had great older neighbors who I befriended. I always loved to be friends with older adults. Perhaps I was missing my parents, retired and living in Mexico.

I became skillful at other things besides sales. I learned to cut hair by observing, so I could save money by cutting Manny and Manuel's hair. Once I got comfortable, I started cutting my neighbor's hair for $5 and promoted this service at the office. I was up for anything to make extra money for our household. Of course, I also took those opportunities to talk about insurance! We were thrilled that we could afford a new car and purchased a 1987 Nissan Sentra. This was yet another important life lesson. When my boss asked what we had for an interest rate, I didn't even know what he was talking about. He read our contract and told me we were getting charged 22.09% interest! He advised me we had 30 days to search for a lower interest rate. I immediately applied for a new loan and received a 9% loan. I appreciated this education on car buying. He was always guiding me in ways like this. He told me if he had a daughter, she would be like me.

I used my experience to caution my clients about interest rates on their large purchases. Of course, they loved me more for this and I got even more client referrals. I learned the more you help and guide people, the more of their respect you will earn. My clients started bringing me their documents so I could translate them from English to Spanish. I was happy to help and never considered charging for this service.

A neighbor invited me to lunch at Kentucky Fried Chicken and gave me a job offer. He said he would pay me more than I was currently making to translate documents. I said I'd consider it, but I knew there was no way I'd leave my current job. I was loyal to my employer for giving me a chance without experience. I also knew he needed me, so I turned the offer down.

Despite the office being swamped, things were going great. I received my first award from my boss. The award was for "Hanging in There After Others Have Let Go!" Before he hired me, I think he had trouble keeping employees. I never tracked my sales, but I knew I was selling a lot of policies! Without knowing it, I had reached a $1,000,000 production mark in life insurance sales. Upselling was a big part of my success. When I sold car insurance, I offered life insurance. Because I was always honest and never employed pressure tactics, most of my customers said *yes*. I received a small bonus for life insurance sales. I never questioned that, either. Because of how my mom raised me, I was a trusting person.

I was granted US citizenship in 1987. Now I could help my husband get his green card. The next year, he received his legal residence approval. Now we could live in peace and continue working hard for a better life in the United States. We took a trip to Mexico to visit both of our parents. Our small family of three had an exciting car adventure. Manuel drove over 2,000 miles on that trip. Another benefit of my citizenship and Manuel's legal residency was the opportunity to become homeowners. Our first attempt to get approved for a loan on a mobile home was unsuccessful. My brother, Victor, played a crucial role in co-signing for us to purchase a condo, which resulted in our approval. Unfortunately, we also needed $2,000 for a down payment. Our boss agreed to lend us the money for the down payment. In 1989, we became homeowners. We were so happy to reach such a huge milestone. Of course, we paid my employer back as soon as we could. However, there was another obstacle. We didn't know, but the realtor gave us a negative amortization loan with a high interest rate. That meant that if we didn't pay extra on our mortgage every month, the balance would go up! We experienced financial difficulties after that. Those years were tough but the feeling of homeownership made us incredibly proud. We had to be patient. Property values started dropping and we couldn't move. Sadly, our neighborhood was horrible. When we bought the condo, our realtor told us it was safe. "You can even leave your car open at night," she assured us. After that, I learned to do my homework and not trust anyone's word in business. I vowed to work hard for a lovely house in a safe area. I continued dreaming of a time when our family could live peacefully. I dreamed about not having to check that our cars were still there. Meanwhile, we protected ourselves until property values increased.

Finally, the five-year hiring commitment to not have more children had passed, and I was pregnant with our second child. I appreciated the job, but it was wrong of my employer to make that a requirement. It was important to me to keep my promise and wait it out. I hoped I could work less before we had any more children. I loved my career, and I knew that wouldn't happen. Ultimately, everything turned out well. As my due date approached, my boss's wife asked for a list of friends to invite to my shower. I said, "WHAT?"

She was excited and said, "Yes, Alice, I am planning a shower for you at my home."

"Wow, how awesome!" I answered. I couldn't believe she was going to do this for us. Manny, my son, was invited to be the special guest for the shower, and he was just as excited as me. He kept telling us he wanted a baby sister and now the time was almost here. We got busy preparing and decorating her bedroom with all the fun things. It was a prayer come true for our growing family. We could not wait to meet her. One morning dawned around 5 am with distinct labor pains and then my water broke. Nervously, I woke Manuel up to tell him it was finally time! He called the doctor, but we were surprised when he told us to stay home until my labor progressed. I was concerned because my water had already broken. The doctor calmly instructed us to put a towel on the mattress and just wait. We decided not to wait! Manuel took Manny to my sister's house and then we headed to the hospital. I called my boss to say I couldn't come to work on

Monday due to the baby's arrival. He and his wife visited us, and once again, made me feel special.

I loved my two months at home with my baby girl. As a mom, returning to work made me feel sad and guilty about leaving her. However, the practical side of me knew I was bettering our family's future. Doing the best for my family was always my motivation to continue pushing myself. Every morning as I prepared for work, I'd reflect on my statement of purpose, my calling, and my conviction. Despite the heavy workload and accompanying stress, it did not matter. My commitment and enthusiasm towards my daily tasks fulfilled me. I enjoyed the responsibility of achieving my goals and the company's mission. I wanted to continue growing at the agency and knew I was there, making a difference. Honestly, this made me feel extraordinary. I often pondered, *What would my boss do without me?* Manuel is the one who witnessed the stress I put myself under, striving to meet the needs of my clients. Each day, I strived for improvement. I learned to stay focused and separate my personal life when needed. When I walked into the office, I blocked out any negativity from what I may be going through personally.

I always thought of my clients as friends. I received invitations from my clients to be a godmother and even attended their special events multiple times. Usually, Manuel would come along as my date. The absence of social life in my youth made me cherish my customers and consider them friends. Interacting with them and solving their problems gave me immense satisfaction. I was passionate about helping people and giving them a smooth, enjoyable experience. Hearing positive feedback from my customers and hearing their appreciation kept me motivated. Every day, I strove to deliver exemplary customer service.

My work schedule was 9-5 weekdays with weekends off. How thankful I was for that! When I wasn't in the office, I was home with my family. That special time meant a lot to us for family bonding. Our Saturdays were laundry day; our kids loved it since we ate donuts at the laundromat. On Sundays, we went to church, had breakfast, and visited the swap meet. Sometimes, I'd look in the newspaper for local events to take the kids to for fun.

A successful career as a wife and mother requires special skills and involvement from everyone at home. We included everyone and never left out a household member. You need to consider everyone because we each have unique needs. Each member of the household sacrifices for a better lifestyle. Of course, it's never easy. It takes a passion for one's career, happiness at your job, lots of love, and communication with your family. But you will reap rewards as you and your family grow. Balancing priorities is key to having both a fulfilling family life and a successful career. Remain flexible to changes that arise. Achieve harmony between family and career by managing your time, seeking support, and being true to yourself. I always remembered I was building a better future for our children. You teach children how to grow as individuals, but they will also imitate how you behave, act, and perform. As parents, they look up to us, whether good or bad. We took being excellent role models seriously. I reminded myself of this often: *You are building a good work ethic and character; never forget that.* I could feel myself more powerful with each new day.

Chapter Six

DETERMINED TO RISE

After nine years at my job, my boss shocked me by announcing a cut in my hours. To my knowledge, he wasn't reinvesting agency profits. He had hired no staff besides me but insisted he could no longer afford me. Telling me it was nothing I had done wrong was not a comfort. It shocked me because I knew I was generating a lot of business, and the company was performing exceptionally well. Our customers loved me—their referrals were pouring in. How could he not afford me after everything we had accomplished? I felt heartbroken and confused. I didn't understand how he could do this to me. I cried, especially since he had always said I was the daughter he never had. This felt like I was losing a family member because that's how his family embraced me. They always were welcoming. Now, I had no choice but to work somewhere new. His lovely son referred me to an agency owner on the other side of town. This was the only person in our community who could afford me. He wasn't writing enough policies and my boss's son said the man was in trouble with his district manager.

When the word got out that my current boss was reducing my hours, I received many job offers. However, I took his son's recommendation. The agency owner I met with had been in business for 18 years. During our interview, I suddenly became emotional about everything I was going through and cried. I felt I didn't deserve the treatment I was receiving after giving the job my all. I treated that business like it was my own, but I understood I was only an at-will employee.

My potential new employer admitted he could not keep employees and loved that I had nine years of experience. His words made me anxious, and I wondered, *Why?* I came right out and asked him. He said quietly, "I have high expectations; I am a hard worker, I'm disciplined, and I'm very strict."

I replied, "That's great! I will excel at this job because I am experienced in working independently, but collaborative teamwork is something I am particularly passionate about. Working with clients is my favorite thing. Your high expectations are music to my ears. I'm open to coaching and receptive to instructions. I'm great at taking ownership."

He liked what he heard, and with my excellent reputation, he hired me on the spot. He placed me on a probationary period for 60 days. During this trial period, he would see if he could afford me at $11 per hour. I accepted his offer. If he saw he couldn't afford me, I asked him to let me know as soon as he could. I did not like job hopping, and I had received many other offers. That shy, insecure little girl was gone. I knew my worth and believed in myself. My insecurities were a thing of the past.

My mom and dad were visiting us from Mexico. I was thrilled to come home with the news that I got hired. My mom said, "Oh no, don't get so excited; wait to see what Manuel says." She didn't know I wasn't worried about what he would say. He always showed me total support.

I started my new job in May 1994, in his tiny office with no coffee maker or microwave. I loved problem-solving and started heating my homemade burritos on my car's dashboard. The burrito was wrapped in foil, placed in a plastic bag, and left to warm in the sun on my dash. It was nice and toasty for my lunch break. It was a brilliant idea! Eventually, we got a microwave for the office. In my excitement, I started a bag of popcorn but forgot to check on it. While was helping a customer, I forgot all about it until it began to burn! How embarrassing. My boss was mad when I confessed what I had done. He refused my offer to replace the microwave and fortunately, we could eventually clean it out enough to use it again.

Those first weeks at my new job were a huge adjustment. The pace was so slow that I would fall asleep. I was used to a fast-paced environment, and this office was too tranquil. There were no walk-ins and no phone ringing. I needed action, so I asked my boss for a yellow-page phone book directory. I started cold-calling people from the phone book. Instead of being high-pressure on the phone, I was conversational. I wouldn't push them toward anything specific. It just felt good to help our community. I wrote out my script, which came directly from my heart. Since cold calling could be tedious, I made it fun! It was an unfamiliar experience. There was never a need to cold-call at my previous job. There, I had plenty of referrals every single day. But now my goal was to bring clients in to purchase insurance and keep me busy. My dynamic positive energy had to be used somehow!

The people I talked with truly listened, resulting in lots of sales. My boss was stunned by my initiative and go-getter attitude. He loved it! These new customers started referring me to their friends and family. The word was out. People began spreading the word, and the referrals started pouring in. This continued for a year, but still, I only received an hourly wage, no bonuses, and no commissions. Although I never asked for a raise, he increased my pay by $1 an hour because of my customer service. I was grateful for a job, so I never questioned him. It wasn't long before he realized I needed a private office. After all, he had great business sense, so he moved us to a bigger office in the same building. He continued to be thrilled and surprised by my work.

When I got my own office, I was incredibly proud of myself. Now, I could make more friends, and that meant more sales. I took the time to educate my clients about the kinds of insurance we offered. I was always sincere in my tone. I explained the contract details because this was something few people understood. Of course, this made my clients love me more. They were referring new clients to me every single day. There was a day when my boss mentioned I was spending too much time with his customers. Later, he apologized when he saw my production and realized I was taking his agency right to the top. With time, our workload increased, and he realized the need for additional staff. When we began interviewing, I was shocked to find out that I was getting an assistant. I felt euphoric. Wow, my own assistant! Everyone, especially my friends, started thinking it was my agency, not his.

A prominent builder in our community contacted me for rates. He was planning a new housing track and was shopping for quotes. He was so happy with my numbers that he said he would refer all his clients to me. Initially, I was speechless, but then thanked him over and over. I felt such gratitude. His referrals would bring in lots of new business for my employer. I still felt it was okay that I wasn't getting rewarded with bonuses or commissions. The way I saw it, this was all part of my hourly pay. We continued to be very busy, even with the extra staff my boss had brought on. Everything was going well.

Then, I got a big surprise. I was going to be a mama again! When I told my boss, he initially had a scared look on his face, but he congratulated me. He later confessed his nervousness about running the business without me during my maternity leave. Thankfully, I had a healthy and comfortable pregnancy. I treasured this time as my last pregnancy. Nothing interfered with my daily responsibilities. I continued to work hard, make sales, and be there for my customers and coworkers. Pregnancy didn't justify slowing down. I was always considerate to schedule my doctor's visits before work at 9:00 a.m.

Every workday at home while pregnant, I'd get up at 5:00 a.m. and pack Manuel his lunch. Around 6:00 a.m., we woke the kids, and he left for work. Manny, now 12, was the first to rise. Stephanie was three. Manny was very good at helping me watch his little sister so I could shower, shampoo, and shine every morning. I never went to work looking unpolished. I always looked professional. We all worked as a team and struggled together. It may not have been easy, and we all sacrificed a lot, but it was okay. We could handle it! We expected each person to do their part. In retrospect, I realize God always aided us. As a landscaper, Manuel started much earlier in the morning than I did. He picked up Stephanie from childcare and made sure Manny did his homework as soon as he got home. Manny walked home from school and we trusted him because he was very responsible.

Knowing it was our last child, I took two weeks off before my due date. I had little Stephanie home with me during the day. It was wonderful to be there when Manny got home from school. I had dinner ready for Manuel when he came home, and we ate together as a family. Although brief, being a stay-at-home mom was a delightful treat. On January 18, little Jordan joined our family. Once Jordan was born, I stayed home as long as I could. Back then maternity leave was just a short six weeks. With my two additional weeks before Jordan came, I was out of the office for eight weeks. Technically, I was on leave, but my boss called me daily with questions. Clearly, he was lost and didn't seem able to run the office without me there. Initially, I was okay with it, but as the calls became more frequent throughout the day, I became overwhelmed. The phone would ring when I was feeding Jordan or when he was napping. Finally, I just turned the phone off. Despite my willingness to assist, the family needed to come first. My boss was unhappy with me at first, but finally, I think he understood. After all, I wasn't getting paid for my maternity leave and I wasn't getting paid to work from home either. I had to make the sacrifice and leave our baby with our "Comadre," (our babysitter.) She was a very responsible lady and was already babysitting our daughter. She was like family to us, but it was difficult to leave such a small baby.

Soon after returning to work, I hit another obstacle. My boss told me I had to be licensed in auto, home, and life insurance. No one had ever told me! Believe it or not, he complained and wondered why he had to pay for my licensure. I know he would have let me shoulder this expense if I had offered. Oh well, I did not make that offer! That evening, I told Manuel he would have to help with the kids more because I had to study. We sat together to create a workable schedule. I planned to study for an hour every day after dinner. After study time, we'd take the kids for a walk around the neighborhood. Working in the sun all day, my husband reluctantly accompanied my children and me to protect us. We started a new family tradition and made our walks part of our daily lifestyle. Getting fresh air was good for my brain and the family's health. That fresh air made me feel great. Our kids enjoyed it because sometimes we also took them to the park.

The study plan we made had paid off, and before long, I was ready to be tested. The testing center was in Los Angeles and Manuel drove me there. The drive was longer than an hour, and then he waited in the car for three hours. He took a day off solely to drive me. I told myself I had to pass, and I did! This was another example of seeing excellent results when the whole family cooperated. Not long after, I tested for my Life and Disability licenses. Manuel waited in the car at the same location. I felt awful for not passing on my first attempt. But, when I went back a couple of weeks later, I passed! It was a tremendous relief and a big load off my shoulders.

Now that I had my license, I expected a raise, but my salary remained the same. Honestly, I did not know the revenue I was producing for his agency. I saw that he bought a new house, cars, and jewelry. His success grew, and I was happy for him and his wife. Once, after he returned from a district meeting, he told me his peers had congratulated and applauded him. He admitted to them it was me who was producing so much. That's when I realized how my sales helped him become a Topper Club, Championship, and President's Council member. He had never shared exactly how that worked. Later, the executives acknowledged him and showcased his picture on the office wall.

He mentioned other agents he thought shared too high a percentage of his life insurance commissions with me. I asked, "Did you tell them I bring you all the home and auto business too, and that you only pay me for the life insurance policies?" He stayed quiet and walked away. Life insurance sales were my only source of commission because they were the hardest to sell. I am so glad I finally started thinking of my family and sticking up for myself. Without specifically planning for it, I had already built a strong reputation in the community and the real estate industry. I was completely unaware of how important this was. In my mind, I was simply providing excellent customer service without expecting a lot of money in return. His agency was HIS business, and I understood that.

I planned to ask permission to pick Stephanie up from school and bring her to the babysitter. My little girl was starting school, and I wanted to be a part of it. I was getting a half-hour lunch break and asked if I could get a 45-minute break instead. Because I always wanted to be fair, I offered a compromise. I offered to solicit home insurance business on weekends (on my time) with local Real Estate offices. Who could resist that offer? It worked out for both of us.

About a year later when we needed a larger house, I asked for a raise. We really needed more space with three children. His response was a question back. He wanted to know why he should pay the consequences because I wanted to spend more money! He offered to think about it and talk it over with his wife. Fortunately, he agreed to pay me $1 more per hour. Let me tell you, I was feeling pretty stressed out and told him it was time he hired more staff. Can you believe he claimed I was stressed because I decided to be? What an ungrateful comment. This negativity toward me started a growing resentment. I started daydreaming about leaving his agency and starting one of my own.

Finally, he hired more staff—I needed help badly. The most challenging part was training them in customer service and sales. Employees would quit or not return after seeing our office's business pace. Despite the challenges, I always respected my customers because I loved helping people. I felt they deserved excellent and knowledgeable service. It was not their fault if we didn't have enough staff. Respect is the reason why clients never see me upset or have a poor attitude. Almost every customer I worked with would refer me to their family and friends. Being bilingual gave me many more opportunities. I always guided my clients on accident claims and educated them on their policies. Because Spanish-speaking clients reminded me of my parents, I went the extra mile to help them. I taught clients the process of taking accident notes. With my guidance, they understood the importance of obtaining auto insurance quotes before they bought a car. I loved talking to their kids and giving them good advice when they started driving.

One day at the office, my boss emotionally said he did not deserve the success I was bringing to his business. I told him there was no reason to feel that way. He should just share his success with me! I laughed awkwardly, and he just walked away. The more time passed, the more he could not believe how quickly I was building his business. Ironically, everyone thought it was my agency, so they always tried to help me. They felt like I needed the support, so they wanted to lend a hand. The amount of work I had was a blessing for my boss. My friends were trying to motivate me to start my own agency. Since my boss did little but read the newspaper in his office, he clearly felt comfortable that I was handling everything well. Unconsciously, I spoiled him, just like I did my other employer. My discipline, motivation, perseverance, and tenacity made me who I am. I was becoming a genuine leader. I am very proud of myself for not wasting my time complaining. Instead, I absorbed all the knowledge I learned along the way and continued to shine brighter than my challenges.

Chapter Seven

MY WHY

I truly enjoyed my 9-5 schedule. I woke up at 5:00 to make Manuel's lunch, wake the kids, and drop them off at school before work. Every evening, I would cook for the family. I didn't feel guilty about being away from home. Our family's legacy was being built day by day. That was my *WHY*. It brought me joy to feed my family and continue building our future. Giving up was never an option!

When I started at this agency, my boss was proud that he had over 2,000 policies. He demanded immediate help when he called the Policy Service staff for assistance. I heard him say it so often that it stuck in my mind. Eventually, he mentioned he was tired and had reached a point where he couldn't grow his business anymore. In eight short years, his portfolio grew to 7,000 policies, and he was incredibly successful. I am thankful for the opportunity he gave me. But did I ever feel appreciated? Sad but true, I didn't feel appreciated at all. Honestly, sometimes I felt like he saw me as the competition! We lacked teamwork even though we were on the same side. I still question why it had to be that way.

Manuel came home from work one day all excited because he had the chance to start his own landscaping company. I wanted to support him, as he always supported me. I had lunch with his supervisor and gave her an insurance estimate for the Southern California stores. What a thrill; we agreed to do business together. I also started to help Manuel with keeping his books. In his first year of self-employment, he did great. His success led me to ask him if he thought he would get more accounts if I opened my own agency. In his usual supportive style, he said, "Of course, yes! I think you are ready. Go for it!" He said, "The other option is to stay where you are and keep growing someone else's business. You've planted many trees on land that is not yours. You leave, and he keeps the trees. It's okay though. Whatever you decide, I will support your decision." Because Manuel was in control, I felt assured to hear his thoughts. I chose not to worry about our finances.

We were both 40 years old, and I had worked for other top-producing agencies for 17 years. I agreed it was time to start my agency. My son Manny was 19 years-old, and it was the perfect time to build our legacy and achieve greatness.

The idea of becoming an entrepreneur excited me. Of course, I felt scared and nervous, but the joy about what the future held was stronger than the fear. Before we could start planning, I had to raise the courage to tell my boss the news. I told him, "I have helped you for many years. You are all set here. I am leaving." To my surprise, he cried.

His first words were, "How much money do you want?" As he continued crying, I explained that my decision was not about the money. It was about doing something grand for my family.

This big life step would require me to depend on both friends and family for their support. I knew they would. I found a cute, little office in downtown Oxnard in the Mayor's building for only $650 a month. It only needed a new paint job to be ready to go. Manuel helped me make it beautiful. My funds were limited, so I got creative. I borrowed my son's computer, bought a fax machine, and thrifted my furniture. I found a white couch for $50 and a great desk for $100. It was time to plan my ribbon cutting and open house.

I received so much love from friends. They brought me gifts, crucifixes, and paintings for my office, ensuring its blessing and removal of negative energies. I invited the mayor and the local newspaper, VIDA, to attend the opening.

When I met with the paper's owner, I was excited to tell him I was starting my business. He said, "With your dynamic personality, you will be a gigantic success in our community. We need leaders like you." My heart overflowed with joy. Who wouldn't love to hear that? I invited the Priest from my church, who said he would be honored to attend. I asked him because of my culture's traditions—having my office blessed was a big deal for me. The open house was on April 1, 2002. My friends created my open house flyer. We served pastries, coffee, atole (rice pudding dink), and pan dulce. It was a hit!

After leaving my job, I felt relieved and born again! I relished that feeling. Instead of support, my former boss treated me as an enemy. He made sure a contract was put in place so I couldn't take his customers. He was paranoid! This contract gave him the rights to my commissions if I sold his clients another type of policy. I chose to fully honor that agreement. However, I had to decline to help people that were his customers. Unfortunately, some people thought it was my decision. They thought now that I was self-employed, I thought I was too good for them. Of course, that was never my intention. I've always believed we humans are all on the same level. This situation made me very sad. Ironically, his decision just made me stand out even more to the people of my community. I would not quit and fought and prayed every day as soon as I opened my eyes. I knew I could beat what was a tremendous challenge because God was on my side.

As I built my agency, it became harder for him to accept that I was no longer building his company. Even though this drama broke my heart and made me cry, I knew I could sell more than him. I picked myself up because my family and clients needed me. How could I allow anyone to control me? I called my friends and hearing their support would give me the energy I needed to keep going. I truly appreciated them—some became my mentors, especially Jorge De Leon, a professional in our community. He had excellent ideas and always said I could call him, and he would gladly listen. Of course, I took advantage. We became good friends and our families did too.

Our district manager at the time was an extraordinarily dedicated human being. Seeing my potential, he supported me 100%. This man was one of my best cheerleaders. He saw I struggled to pass my 6 and 63 Financial Services Licensing and took the time to tutor me. His assistant, an innovative and bright lady named Marie, also became my friend and was great at cheering me up. I love people, so the more positivity they poured into me, the better. I believe in angels, and I know many of them surrounded me.

Just imagine my juggling act. I was starting a business from scratch. I needed to meet sales quotas, raise three kids, be a wife, deal with my ex-boss's financial issues, and, on top of that, study stock trading. When I look back, I know it was God who guided me. Who else could it have been? I could have taken the easy road and given up many times over. But my faith had carried me all my life, thanks to my mom. She taught me that God listens because He is alive.

A local insurance agent, Joe, heard how much I was struggling, and offered me his office to process my policies. My assistant and I wrote out policies during the day and processed them on his computers after work. We did that for about six months. Again, I struggled, but I did not quit.

My family's financial security was at stake if I failed the licensing test. I had received various job offers, so I knew I wouldn't be jobless. Manuel reassured me and proposed moving to Arizona as an alternative. *No way!* I whispered in my head. *I'm not a quitter! I know God will help me.* I prayed and prayed and prayed and would fall asleep studying— those were some tough years for me.

As I mentioned, my district manager offered to tutor me, and it helped a lot. I remained focused. He told me I was skipping words and going too fast. I chuckled when I admitted to having a lot on my plate. I told him I was feeling anxious and didn't feel I could take breaks. He laughed too. Thankfully, God listened to my prayers. After six months of praying and studying between sales and service clients, I passed! I believe God helped every step of the way. He knew it was for a good cause, and my struggle was worth the cost. Finally, I had peace and felt relieved to be me again. I was so grateful because I knew when I achieved that milestone, my dream of helping my Hispanic community would come true. Many people in my community didn't know how to invest their money. I promised to offer them products to help them to the best of my ability. And I did just that.

I received a call from the corporate office stating that a Financial Services Representative was assigned to help me with my securities and investment sales. That was perfect! Now, I could be sure my clients would be helped in the right way. I didn't want to make a mistake or make a bad investment for them. I treated their investments as if they were mine. Clients would ask me to invest their savings however I wanted. I never did that. They needed to make the choice and learn about the products for themselves—it was their decision, not mine. Of course, I felt exceptional that I had earned their trust.

I had received full approval and had my very own password and log in. Now my assistant Ivonne and I could focus day and night on sales. We were both so happy. Those were good days indeed. Finally, I felt the freedom of being self-employed. I eagerly spread the word about how I could help people. I was invited to join different organizations. I joined the Hispanic Chamber of Commerce, The Ventura County Realtor Association, the BNI group, and Toastmasters. Maria, a friend in Real Estate, invited me to join The National Association of Hispanic Real Estate Agents. I love the mission of this organization in its commitment to instilling passion, a love for entrepreneurship, and advocating for cultural heritage. I became a member of the board. It was the best thing I had done until that point. I met amazing people and achieved professional growth for myself. Everyone welcomed me. I love their mission, which was to help advance sustainable Hispanic homeownership.

Being a caring empathetic person, I wanted to help this organization grow. I tried to attend every monthly meeting. One way I helped was by providing lunch and getting reimbursed later. If you think of others before yourself, you will reap rewards sooner rather than later. Just be responsible, truthful, and honest. Remember, your character speaks louder than words. Your work ethic should remain consistent within and outside your business. And don't forget, having a good attitude is always a plus.

I also believed even though I was a small business, I could think like a big corporation. I started donating and sponsoring events, especially the ones that referred business to us. A local body shop called and asked me to donate six months of auto insurance to a family in need. Without a doubt, I enthusiastically said *yes*! With less than a year in the business, I was excited to lend a hand. I felt it was time to give back to the community as much as I could.

My district manager had a tradition for his new agents. He would celebrate their first $10,000 paycheck. To my surprise, my check came in before my first anniversary. I organized a "happy hour" at a popular restaurant, "Cabo," downtown. My staff, family, clients, executives, and business partners attended the celebration. It was the first of many to come.

Walking into my office daily fueled my love for my work and assisting others. It also helped that I could be myself 100% of the time. Manuel played a major role in my success. Having him by my side always allowed me to focus on my sales, clients, etc. Our office had an alley, so I would call him to come pick me up when I stayed late. I usually left around 7:00 p.m. He would sometimes complain and say, "You are tired and won't think as clearly today. Leave it for tomorrow." But mostly, he understood. Your success will be limited if you don't have a partner who cooperates with your dreams and goals. This applies to every business. A family needs to be united and help each other without jealousy or selfishness. If you know and remember your *WHY*, it benefits everyone.

I celebrated my first business anniversary by thanking everyone for their referrals and support. This began a tradition to celebrate yearly by inviting our business partners to my office to network. I always took a flyer to local offices and asked them to stop by for coffee, juice, and pastries. I emphasized they could pop in and out because I knew they were busy. Usually, there was a great turnout!

Manuel met an older couple through his business who made fresh tamales daily on banana leaves. They were delicious and had the perfect spice: pork, chicken, beef, and cheese. We bought plenty for our open house party celebration every year—they were a hit! Everyone loved them. After that, we purchased them monthly and delivered them to our business partners. My husband always came along. He would be my "chauffeur" while I dropped them off, mingled, and chatted at their offices. I loved to see them. Our monthly route comprised approximately thirty offices, all within Ventura County. We started getting famous with the tamales. Our business colleagues would call my office to get the "tamale guy" information. Those were great times! I was busy, but happy to help the tamale guy sell more. I always wanted to support my business associates.

Sometimes we were so busy we didn't take a lunch break. I'd tell Ida to go to lunch, but she'd wait until the office calmed down. Her hard work and dedication did not go unnoticed. I came up with, *"I buy you fly"* for lunch. Our favorite spot was right next door at La Rancherita Restaurant. We took turns eating so our office would always be open. We dealt with stress by laughing. OMG, we made it fun. With her help, we sold over 1,500 policies in my first year. I had no idea I was breaking sales records at the National level.

I was determined not to let the challenges and adversities from my previous employer hurt me. Proving I could build my agency without his help was my adrenaline to keep going strong. I'm sure he saw my production more than anyone. My work left a powerful impression on my district manager. He told me that I was exceptional and predicted a bright future for me. He'd say, "Just wait. You will celebrate more when you see the renewal premiums." I did not know how this business worked! No one shared that side with me. With time, my gratitude increased. Eventually, I could not believe my eyes with what began to develop for my business.

My recommendation? Never start an insurance business just to make money. Instead, build a business because you enjoy everything that comes with it, from gaining product knowledge to dealing with unique client personalities, practicing patience, maintaining discipline, demonstrating perseverance, and showing empathy when filing a claim. You will have good days and bad days. Focus on the good, forget the bad. Each day presents a chance to improve and grow from errors. Your positive attitude is a must. Never forget that.

Whenever I needed a notable boost, I'd call my mom in Mexico. Simply hearing her voice was enough for me. I'd share my wins, and she would be so proud of me. One day, she told me, "No matter how famous and how many millions you get, never stop being humble."

I laughed. "Millionaire! I can only imagine."

Her comment stayed in my head; I thought my momma would be very proud if I ever reached the top. I had to show her that even though she had little faith in me growing up; I made it. After that, she became my number one fan! My mom was the first love of my life. With her presence and support, I would have the peace I needed to continue following my dreams. I wanted to make her proud. Despite her distance, she was still a vital part of my motivation to continue. I included her in every celebration, every award, and every recognition.

I took the time to inspect some homes with my husband on our lunch break one day. He told me, "You need to get some fresh air. Let's have lunch together. We can inspect some of my jobs." As we drove by a lovely neighborhood, there was an Open House for a home for sale. It was so beautiful. I told my husband, "Let's go see it." We loved it! Manuel, usually conservative, agreed to take a look. It was very close to the office, so we could come and go within five minutes. We were working seven days a week those days. I called the Realtor, but he reported the house had already sold. We continued looking and found another home we liked. I called my friend, who was a realtor in Mexico, and she referred us to her aunt in the US. We made an offer, and they accepted it. This was a big deal since my agency was new and my husband had only been self-employed for a while. We could not believe this milestone. Again, we both knew it was God. I couldn't wait to share the news with Mom. I was so excited—I could barely talk. I said, "Mom, we bought another house, and we want you and Dad to visit us!"

Nervously, she said, "Are you going to be able to pay for it?"

I said, "Yes, Mom! Please don't worry!"

A few months later, they traveled from Mexico to visit us. What a joy! We prepared a welcoming barbeque and invited my siblings. Mom was so happy to be here. She loved living in America, but Dad refused to live here. His hard labor many years ago made him decide to live in Mexico. Plus, the cost of living in Mexico provided a better lifestyle for them. Mom never learned how to drive. Moroleon was so small she could walk everywhere, especially to church. She donated her time volunteering with jail inmates. She had a big heart and truly enjoyed helping people in need. When I struggled with sales and the responsibilities of entrepreneurship, I'd call her. She was great at listening. One day, back when I first opened my business, I was desperate, and said, "Mom, please pray for me." I cried; I was hurting badly.

She said, "What's wrong?"

I said, "I couldn't pass my test, and my ex-boss wanted me to get fired. I've been audited a couple of times, and that is not normal. It was probably him. I have nothing to hide, but it feels horrible to think the company may not trust me."

She responded, "Don't worry, I won't just pray, but I will tell the Priest to honor you with a Mass."

Immediately after she said that I felt so much peace in my soul. I could go back to work and continue to hustle! Deep inside, I had faith and believed everything would work out. From that conversation, I created this mantra: *If I allow myself to be happy, I can inspire others to be happy as well.*

When I helped a customer and saw that they were struggling for whatever reason, I told them what worked for me. Most of the time, my positivity helped them, and that made me happier. It was a wonderful feeling when a customer left my office in a better state than when they arrived. Their loyalty to me was something I will always cherish. Hopefully, because of me, they learned there is good in the world, just like I had learned.

Chapter Eight

FULFILLING DREAMS

In 2004, I received my first Topper Club Achievement invitation, an award for my agency ownership, and Rookie Agent of the Year 2003. My district manager ensured that Farmers Insurance saw my production. I also received invitations to numerous events to encourage others to become insurance agents. Even though I was a business owner, Farmers Insurance also contracted me. That meant I was required to follow all their rules and regulations, or risk being fired as an agency owner. While speaking at our career school, they asked me to share my method for strong sales and retaining customers. I was thrilled with the outcome of this presentation. I became so well-renowned in our community that I felt like a movie star. I'd see my clients everywhere I went and always introduced them to my husband. They showed appreciation when I stopped to say hello. Sometimes, they'd ask for insurance advice, and I'd gladly give it to them. Seeing how much our community trusted me was something I appreciated.

This may sound funny. I was so busy running my business I had no time to look at my production folio. I believed my monthly earnings were accurate. I fully trusted Farmers and had faith that everything was good. I never questioned it. I just saw that I was growing very fast and living my dream. I didn't worry about tracking our sales because I was too busy helping clients and selling. I trusted my district office to do that for me. The Farmers Insurance district office ensures that their agencies adhere to their guidelines. Winning any type of recognition always surprised me. My philosophy was to work hard and always do my best. I knew God would do the rest. God gave me the wisdom to appreciate the people surrounding me. Treat everyone equally and work hard; God will provide. Don't take advantage of others and always be open about your actions for them.

One Sunday morning, I couldn't get out of bed. I yelled for Manuel and told him everything around me was spinning so much I couldn't move. He was frightened and tried to help me walk, but I had to lie back down. It wasn't improving, so he called the doctor and took me to the hospital. The doctor ordered tests to look for high blood pressure, cholesterol, and diabetes. I was relieved that everything came back negative.

The doctor determined that I had vertigo. It affected my inner ear and caused the imbalance I was experiencing. The doctor told me that vertigo is stress-related and ordered me to join a gym and start working out. When I pushed back, complaining that I was needed in the office, he became short with me. He said, "If you don't care for your health, there will be no business! You could die from a heart attack." I agreed to take time off but was uneasy about being home. This was a wake-up call for me and I hired additional staff.

It wasn't easy finding the right staff for this fast-paced environment who were passionate and believed in my office culture. I always held the interviews hoping to motivate and inspire applicants. I told my customers I was looking for staff and about my expectations. That's how I met Alex. Alex was a sweet client of mine who worked for the County. She told me about a unique program that referred people who had issues getting a job. Alex referred me to Karen, a hardworking and smart addition to our staff. We loved her, and she loved us. She had the empathy I was looking for and outstanding customer service skills. Once I found a good team member, I tried to mentor and make them feel special. I not only shared my experience, but I also shared bonuses and compensation. I appreciated my team and didn't want to appear better than anyone else in the office. Clients' expectations for fast and accurate service posed challenges for new employees. I continued to look for another part-time employee to round out our office. Keeping everyone motivated and finding time for mentoring was an ongoing, challenging task. I realized most people wanted everything easy and weren't willing to work for success. Just as my former bosses were patient with me, I now was patient with my staff. I told myself I would take care of them way better than my employers had taken care of me. The experiences I had previously helped me a lot in this process.

Manuel and I decided it was a good time to purchase an investment property. Before I became self-employed, we had sold a property in Moroleón that we bought from my parents. We used the funds from that sale to buy an affordable duplex in Taft, CA. We wanted a financial cushion in case my business didn't work out. It gave us peace of mind so that we could do what was necessary to build my new agency. The decision was a blessing because we had excellent tenants, and had one less thing to worry about. Manuel was the handyman, collected the rent, and did all the maintenance.

As always, I was grateful for my Manuel. I appreciated how he helped with all the outside marketing and home inspections so I could stay at the office. As we became even busier at home and the office; we had to decide…either his business or mine. After negotiating, we sold his business. I offered him the chance to help me full-time. Manuel had given up his own business for mine. At first, it was difficult, because I had become his boss. In our culture, the male is mostly the breadwinner, so it took time for him to accept this new reality. He also continued to help at home and with the kids. This included school rides, house chores, being my chauffeur, and anything he could do at the office. Manuel did everything but sales. Salesmanship did not interest him. I was just thankful he was okay with all the other duties he had on his plate. He even tried to learn to cook, but we quickly realized I was better in the kitchen! I made dinner right after I left the office. Sometimes, I'd cook for two days, and we learned to eat leftovers. We had so many new sales that it created long lists of home site visits for Manuel to inspect. I gave him the title of Marketing Specialist. He wouldn't share the fact that he was my husband with our clients and that avoided unnecessary conversations. Manuel was constantly in a hurry to complete site visits because he had to pick up the kids from school. He always gave 100% to his responsibilities.

The home office enjoyed motivating us with special sales promotions. The newest was a personal lines promotion that included auto and home insurance. Because we never stopped in our office and loved sales so much, we won this new promotion. The reward was a seven-day train trip through the Canadian Rockies. This was one luxurious experience I will never forget. Manuel and I flew to Canada from the LA airport and a courteous guide met us. He drove us to the train station, and we were treated like royalty. Seeing those mountains and breathing the clean air was an unbeatable experience. Every night, we would stop at a different five-star hotel to spend the night. The next day, we would board the train again.

At 20 years old, Manny had become a good-looking, dynamic, and responsible young man. He wanted to join the agency. I conducted a formal interview like I would do for any potential new hire. I explained that while at the office; he was not my son. Like every employee, he had to hustle, earn respect, follow my rules, and respect our office culture. He agreed to follow my direction and took the job seriously. At first, he struggled with working behind a desk. I had him trained by Ivette (my office manager at the time), not myself. I felt he would try harder if someone other than myself trained him. I told him he must start at the bottom and work his way up. He tried very hard. He learned to love this career and realized it wasn't just another job. We watched him become very passionate about insurance. I began introducing him to our business partners and associates. Everyone welcomed him and shared their knowledge, and he soon grew into a professional. I mentored him and helped shape him into a fantastic insurance agent – a mini-me! Just listening to him talk to our clients was a dream come true. My legacy was becoming a reality. He earned our clients' respect, and for that, I was grateful.

Chapter Nine

TRUE CHAMPION

In 2005, I was finally eligible to qualify for an invitation to our Championship convention. The feeling was great since the invitation was under my name. I was the true champion. Woohoo! Now, it was my turn. I began loving this business more and more. The company invited me to travel to Cancun and enjoy a stay at a beautiful five-star resort. Instead of having complete joy for this accomplishment, worry immediately set in. I had concerns for my kids and clients during my absence.

This Cancun event was my first convention, and I knew I would get to meet our Top Insurance champions and executives. To feel and look good, I informed Manuel it was time for me to get in shape. I started looking for personal trainers at my local gyms. I received a recommendation that was perfect for me. We'd meet at 5:00 a.m. for 30 minutes, and I paid $500 a month. Never in my dreams did I think I could afford such an expense! However, it was worth it, and

I'm glad I did it. My trainer was a brilliant coach. I lost a few pounds, learned new techniques, and felt great!

Before we left, I went shopping and found a perfect gala gown and a nice suit for Manuel. We were ready to live the experience. How exciting! A deluxe shuttle picked us up at the airport in Cancun to take us to the hotel. The staff was waiting for us when we arrived and went out of their way to make us feel special. It was an incredible experience. I always made sure Manuel was involved in all my competitions and all the trips when I won. He was on my "planning committee" and was the perfect person for it. He had great time management and organizational skills—he was my right hand. I became more comfortable delegating at the office and trusting Manny and my sister to watch the kids.

We received an agenda for the event, from workshops to free time and awards celebration. The more seasoned agents greeted us on the awards night. We started with a cocktail hour, followed by an elegant dinner and special entertainment. Our seats were in a special section for first-time champions. We waited for our names to be announced, and the other agents enthusiastically welcomed us. Instantly, I resolved to do what it took to guarantee a yearly invitation. It was beautiful gratification for all our hard work. We could see that Farmers Insurance truly appreciated us.

I started a new tradition when I got back to the office. I would share what I learned at every event with my staff, and we would put it into practice immediately. I shared office sales promos with them and always included my team. At home, I made sure we took our kids on trips so they wouldn't feel left out. My elderly parents were on my list too. No matter how much work I had to do, we planned a family trip to see them in Mexico. Sometimes Manuel drove us over 2,000 miles to see them. Fortunately, he loves to drive. I am blessed and thankful for that. Mom would have lunch or dinner ready for us when we arrived. These were always such great times together. We planned out our destinations and would drive Mom and Dad around, visiting small towns and villages. Mom loved visiting churches to thank God for allowing us to see them and spend quality time together. Now, this is my tradition and my husband's as well. Mom and Dad always looked forward to our annual visits. Sometimes, we would visit when the kids were out of school and around my birthday. Mom loved helping me organize birthday parties. She'd contact the siblings in Mexico so they could come to her house to help celebrate. She loved having all of us together. Sometimes we would visit in the winter around Stephanie and Jordan's birthdays. We would celebrate the birthdays together and they got to spend time with their cousins.

Family is essential. They give us the love and energy to continue pursuing our dreams. Never leave them behind, especially your aging parents. You never know when they'll pass from this Earth, leaving only memories.

Chapter Ten

MERCEDES BENZ

We had a sales production competition at the end of 2005. The prize was for the top five agents in our territory to visit New Orleans. This was part of the newly attained Zurich Insurance Company, which sponsored this competition. Guess what? I made it! The news left me speechless with just a "Wow! I got an invitation for a luxurious trip in January during Mardi Gras, with Manuel as my guest. We enjoyed a fancy limo ride from the airport complete with a bottle of champagne. The story our driver shared with us dampened our joy. When Katrina hit New Orleans, he had to leave the city. He felt crushed when he found out that one of his relatives had died in the hurricane. He had to continue working to provide for his family, even though they needed him back home. It was an experience that changed him forever, as it did for so many people caught in Katrina's path. Instead of taking us directly to the hotel, he gave us a tour. New Orleans still resembled a ghost town in many areas. As he talked to us with tears in his eyes, we could see how much he was still hurting. He touched our hearts. After seeing New Orleans through his eyes, we were thrilled to be asked to help build a home in the city. Farmers Insurance offered this as one of their activities during the convention. We jumped at the chance! Among the options given, this one felt like a special gift. We got to contribute to this community when they need it most.

The streets were closed the day after our awards dinner for the Mardi Gras parade. This was the real thing! Farmers Insurance provided a unique experience that we would have never had without their generosity. Each evening, we had cocktails with elegant dinners. Activities and programs filled the three days for those who didn't choose to help build a home.

When we got back to California, we shared our experiences with our family. Together, we prayed for New Orleans. The trip was meant to celebrate success, but I didn't see it that way. I saw an opportunity to aid others and was glad to help. This is one trip I will hold in my heart forever. I never took these trips for granted. They gave me energy, wisdom, camaraderie, and the opportunity to meet more top agents. Also, I was getting stronger to be ready to fight any adversities coming my way.

I received another invitation to the Championship Convention that year. Since it was my second time attending, I knew what to expect. This year, they held the Championship Convention in Arizona at The Phoenician, a Luxury Collection Resort in Scottsdale. Learning that I had earned an award came as a shock to me. This trip included an optional activity as well, so we drove up the mountains in a Jeep. We learned about Scottsdale's history. It was so much fun! On other days, we had workshops and prize drawings, all while constantly learning about our company's new and upcoming procedures.

On award day, we had cocktail hour first, then a luxurious dinner. Our seats were next to some top agents and executives. I could feel butterflies in my stomach and began getting a little anxious. Our table sat directly in front of the stage. They informed me I had won the "Agent of the Year for Personal Lines in the USA." That award changed my life completely. I didn't let it go to my head; momma always told me to stay humble. Colleagues wanted to take pictures with me after receiving the award. I was the first Latina ever to receive that size award. Everyone was so proud of me.

People asked, "How did you do it?"

I'd humbly respond, "I worked hard, and insurance is my life."

"Can I get your business card so we can talk?"

I passed out many, many business cards.

Insurance agents from different parts of the country started coming to my small office in Oxnard. They'd invite me to lunch so I could share my business strategies. They were all eager to know my sales secrets and would ask if I paid for it! I would respond, "Not one penny. All I do is treat every customer with respect and educate them about insurance. They leave my office happy. That's all!" They always expressed surprise that it was so uncomplicated. I told everyone that I loved to share what I knew. When I could, I'd provide a meal to show my appreciation. I always mentioned that I was never lazy, and my clients were always my highest priority. It was my breakout year!

Being nationally recognized as a woman, Farmers Insurance Marketing invited me to an event to be held in Hollywood with Actor Edward James Olmos. He and I were to represent the company at a special HOPE Foundation event. The HOPE Foundation has built a generation of productive women and youth to live their dreams. I was to mentor and inspire them, and I loved it! I had the privilege of doing what I most loved. Part of this celebration was a professional photo shoot for a local magazine. They wrote a beautiful story about me, and the photos were amazing! These are enduring memories.

My sales numbers continued to skyrocket—I couldn't believe it myself. I felt grateful to my family, friends, and business associates. I wanted to share my wins, and what would be better than having a large party to show my appreciation? Before I planned the party, Manuel and Manny told me it was time to give myself a gift.

"What kind of gift," I said.

"Mom, a new 2006 Mercedes Benz."

I said, "What? Let me think about it."

As an immigrant from a modest lower-income household, I had never seen a new luxury car in my future. All I had wanted was an office job, to dress nicely, be well-groomed, and work indoors. But now I could afford a luxury car and I told myself I deserved it. So, I agreed and said, "Let's go shopping for it!" Excitement overtook all of us. I picked out a beautiful black Mercedes Benz. At first, I felt weird driving it, like everyone would stare at me. Later, I fell in love with it.

I discussed my celebration plans with my friends at our next National Association of Hispanic Real Estate Professionals Ventura County (NAHREPVC) meeting. Thankfully, I received lots of volunteers to help me make this party beautiful and memorable. We even had a party planning committee. I couldn't have been happier with the love and support I received. I had about 150 guests at a beautiful venue around Christmas time. We were at the Residence Inn at River Ridge in Oxnard. It brought joy to celebrate with those who supported me. Most of the guests were salespeople. What do salespeople need? Inspiration and motivation! Dr. Mary Barretto was a great office neighbor and family therapist. I invited her to be my motivational speaker, and she was happy to accommodate me. Mary wanted guidance on her topic, but I felt she should choose. Everyone enjoyed her presentation. She was a beautiful lady. We had a lovely dinner. A friend of mine volunteered to photograph the party and be the DJ. My friend, Jorge De Leon, was my event host and ensured everyone had fun. He told jokes; for instance, he told everyone that the parking lot looked like a luxury car dealership, which made everyone laugh. He told my guests I was an insurance icon, not just a Farmers Insurance agent. The comment made me cry. Laughter and love filled the room. I spoke often with my business partners but had yet to meet most of them face-to-face. This party allowed me to meet them for the first time. It was so awesome!

Party over, business boomed! No matter what type of business you have, never be afraid to invest in it. If you give it your heart and soul, you will not lose, trust me. It was essential for clients to be more informed about insurance after leaving my office than they knew when they arrived. My mom advised me to make sure people always said good things about me. Based on that, I taught my clients about the products, gave them options, and had a lot of patience. I didn't care how much money they had—everyone was the same to me. That was part of my office culture. When we trained new staff, they had to share my beliefs; otherwise, things would not work out. I always tried to have a good office climate. If my staff was happy, then they would help our clients better. That is client and employee retention, and that equals growth.

In 2006, my husband and I attended Topper Club, another achievement club. The beautiful city of Miami hosted it. We got to experience Cuban food, especially fried bananas; they were delicious! Every trip I took, I remembered to thank my staff. I truly enjoyed meeting new colleagues, talking to my executives, and sharing how to market and sell more efficiently. I never underestimated these trips. Coming back home, I had new incredible ideas to implement. A key to continuing to produce more business was personally calling our customers to thank them for their loyalty.

Chapter Eleven

HITTING MY STRIDE

The year 2007 marked a turning point in my career. It's every insurance agent's dream to achieve the highest level of production. This requires community involvement, an excellent reputation, and a strong work ethic. The President's Council Club extends invitations to less than 3% of over 20,000 agents nationwide. Amid a busy day at the office, I got a three-way call from my top executives. They were calling to invite me to join them at my very first Presidency Convention. It left me temporarily speechless!

I said, "What!? YES! It will be an honor to attend!"

They said, "Your hard work is not going unnoticed. We would like you and your husband to join us in New York City!"

I found it hard to concentrate and continue working—that's how impressed I was. That invitation impacted me deeply. I believed the goal was still out of my reach. The first person I called was my Manuel, then my momma. They were so happy for me. Mom told me, "Be careful in New York, I heard it's dangerous." That was my momma; always worried about her children. I was so overcome with happiness that I even told my clients about it. Usually, they would stand up and hug me. It was so sweet. I thanked God for His incredible blessing and started getting excited about this incredible experience.

Manuel and I went gown shopping. I found the perfect dress—black and gold. I felt amazing in it! He found a nice black tuxedo. Manuel was in shock as well. He didn't know what he had done to deserve so much. After our shopping trip, we were all set. We had our gala outfits, clothes to wear at the resort, and we had made sure our kids were taken care of. Unfortunately, just days before the convention, I sprained my ankle and couldn't walk. Ugh. How could this happen? There was no way I could attend the convention in this condition, so I took immediate action. I went to the doctor, and he prescribed me steroids. What a relief! I immediately experienced healing. There was no way I was going to miss that convention. Now, we could prepare to go. We flew directly from Los Angeles to New York City. A chauffeur in a black limo was waiting for us. Once we arrived at the

Waldorf Astoria in Manhattan, the staff treated us like royalty. It was a new level of luxury and beauty. I remember asking my husband, "What did we do to deserve this?"

His response was, "Thank you so much for all you do; I am so proud of you!"

The awards ceremony began with a cocktail hour, where we were introduced to seasoned President's Council Club members. The company made sure the convention was both memorable and comfortable enough to share our business practices. We knew we would go home and implement the ideas that would work for us. I also received my first-year surprise—a diamond ring! They added a new diamond each year, as I was invited back. It was such a beautiful and thoughtful surprise. They assigned us a table number for our seating after cocktails. As first-timers, they assigned us to sit near the stage with Top Agents and executives. We were left in awe! The hotel placed a red carpet at the door to walk on when our name was called. At the same time, our production numbers were projected onto the large screen. We took a picture with our CEO and his wife. Everyone clapped. It was such a fantastic experience. And last but certainly not least, our surprise guest was Donna Summer!

While we were in New York, we received tickets to see the play "Mamma Mia" at a beautiful theater. As part of our celebration and acknowledgments, they invited us to the New York Stock Exchange. We got to see our name on the screen outside Wall Street! How cool is that? We had been asked to send a photo of us as a couple before the trip. When we arrived back home, a delivery person brought us a beautiful 16x20 oil painting.

After living this "fairy tale trip," I told myself I had to go back again. Despite the difficulties and challenges of maintaining a business, I went back eight more times! The events were in unique locations like Fajardo, Puerto Rico, Kona, Hawaii, Marco Island, Florida, Scottsdale, Arizona, and West Virginia. We received an invitation to Monte Carlo, Monaco, but COVID-19 forced the cancellation— tough times for all of us.

Our daughter was going to be fifteen in 2007. In our Latin American culture, we celebrate our daughters with a special party called a "Quinceanera" for their 15th birthday. This is a religious and social celebration emphasizing the importance of family and society in the life of a young woman. I mentioned this party to my friends and business associates and immediately began receiving volunteers. My friend Hilda Luna had party-planning experience. She was a total blessing to our family. This party was an opportunity to share a special family night with everyone supportive of us. Gathering our community regularly is vital, because life is more than just work. It's also about having fun and supporting each other. Life is short, and you never know when God will call you to join Him.

I loved organizing the party and practicing the program to make this an excellent show for our guests. I chose a salsa dance called "Carnaval" by Celia Cruz. My daughter had four "chamberlains" teenagers, all dressed in bright-colored shirts, to dance with her. They were amazing! My husband chose "Vals de Las Flores," an extraordinary and classical father-daughter dance. We served Filet Mignon, white and red wine, champagne, and beer. For music, we had a DJ, Trio Guadalajara, and a professional band specializing in salsa music called "Yari More." This party was a hit! Our daughter felt like a beautiful princess with her pink and sparkly long gown. Her chamberlains wore black tuxedos with pink ties. Everyone danced, ate well, and loved it.

We had outgrown our office, so I looked for another location—hopefully somewhere with a storefront. I envisioned hiring agents to help our clients, but I would need more workstations. God heard my prayers, and I found an excellent location, only a few blocks from our current office.

According to my district manager, moving results in a 10% client loss. I knew moving just a short distance would help that percentage go down. The office I found needed some work, and the landlord would not invest one dollar. He said if I wanted it, then it would be my full responsibility. As a risk taker, I believed in myself and agreed to pay for renovations. I paid to have a wall put in to make my office private. I also kept paying for my first office for six more months to ensure my clients could find me. I wasn't taking any chances!

Now, I had a beautiful storefront and a big office. I was very comfortable for both my staff and my clients. I felt fulfilled and began hiring more staff. I called my district manager and asked if he would be interested in a promo for my office. He loved me because he didn't have to push me. I was a natural in sales and always his district leader. Honestly, I loved seeing my name at the top of the production list. I tripled the sales of others in my district most of the time.

Our open house featured our famous banana leaf tamales, pastries, Starbucks, and atole. Our friends supported us and showed us good faith. As a family business, we became even more well-known in our community. The company was blooming more every day. As a family business, we gained a reputation for being highly respected and continued to be so.

It's vital when you have a business to be part of your community. Include them whenever you can. Spread love and greatness. Sponsor youth sports and donate funds. Don't be cheap. Your business would not exist if it weren't for their support.

We continued to be very busy. I was so thankful for my fantastic staff and for how well our children were doing in school. They invited me to celebrate another Championship event in the Bahamas because of our production numbers. That trip was another one-of-a-kind experience. I always returned home with overflowing positive energy. I'd pass it on to my staff, clients, and, of course, to my husband and family at home. I dealt with stress by focusing on the good and seeing how our lives changed because of my business. God blessed us with his many gifts. Being exposed to beautiful parts of the country was enough to help me with any adversity.

Chapter Twelve

OVERCOMING DIFFICULTIES

I had won an auto insurance promotion by Farmers for the agent with the highest sales. They invited me to throw out the first pitch for a classic Dodger vs Angels game at Dodger Stadium. I practiced for a week to ensure I would do well since I was not a baseball player. Along with this honor, they arranged for me to have an interview displayed on the big screen at the stadium, and televised.

I know my success had a great deal to do with the loyalty I've always shown to others. I believed in inspiring others through my solidity and faithfulness. Maybe the reason I never concentrated on my numbers was that I love competing with myself, but not with others. Once you focus on what others are doing more than what you are doing, you lose. With every policy I sold, I reminded myself of what Jesus would do. Would this policy be what they truly needed? I kept that thought in my mind. I am happy to say my conscience was always clear. I would offer clients different benefit options, so they had choices, and I worked within their budget. The business I built was not to meet my needs before others. I served my clients by sharing my wisdom from product knowledge to life experience. My clients were extremely comfortable with me and that's exactly how I trained all my staff. If a policy came back with a higher premium because of weight, I would offer tips so that the next year the premium would go down. My reduced premium because of those suggestions was never an issue. Sometimes, it worked, and I would feel proud of both of us for the achievement.

Referrals were an assurance that we were doing a good job. I loved referrals, and I never had to pay for them. My clients were happy to see how we cared for them—that mattered to them. They knew we would help them to the best of our ability, especially if they only spoke Spanish. Spanish-speaking clients always reminded me of my parents. We would translate their documents and were always willing to go above and beyond. When someone came to see me after hearing good things, I would joke, "I hope they're good." And even if my rate was higher, they would be honest and say, "I'll pay a little more just to be insured by you." It's hard to explain how much that comment always touched my heart. Those compliments made the stress and challenges worth it. Making sure my family and staff were happy was all that mattered to me.

Between 2007-2009, we faced a severe economic crisis known as "The Great Recession" followed by a lengthy and sluggish recovery in America. We lost almost 2,000 clients. We had empathy for everyone who lost their home because of foreclosures. All we could do was give them hope and tell them they would be homeowners again one day. I educated myself on how to guide them correctly. Thankfully, I could gather information from the different real estate organizations I belonged to. I had an enormous responsibility to motivate my staff. I kept everyone employed; they needed me just like I needed them. I believed it would pass. There was no economic profit for us during that period. I poured everything back into the business and to my staff. We all faced challenges during those years. Achievement clubs didn't even cross my mind. All I wanted was to stay afloat. With God's blessings, we continued to move forward.

Our 25th wedding anniversary was approaching, and I had a dilemma. Should we let it pass, or celebrate? Manuel suggested we should not spend the money. I got excited and told him if God had granted us the health and blessings to be together, we should celebrate! I wanted to return to Mexico and gather everyone who had supported us back in 1983 when we were extremely limited in funds. My sister Rosa and her husband Leo, who lived in Mexico, made the party possible. They did all the organizing. This time, my dad was there. I forgave him for not being present on my original wedding day. My mom, family, and friends all attended. Seeing my husband and family celebrating together all night was a dream come true. Thankfully, we could leave our issues in America, at least for a short time.

I believe I was born to overcome setbacks with relative ease. It's a trait called resilience. We can have a greater sense of control over how we respond to what happens in our lives. I've been willing to take risks for this reason. Also, in my case, my optimistic outlook made it easier to develop and maintain positive relationships with others. I tried to make my life meaningful by having a balanced life. How did I do it? I stayed flexible, connected, believed in myself, and believed in God. I embraced healthy habits, released tension, and maintained a positive outlook. It seems like a lot, but everything worked together for the best.

My plan aimed to redirect my staff's attention from lost policies and clients. Instead, try to focus on the opportunity to offer other lines of products. That's precisely what they did. Everyone in my office started looking forward to better times. This downtime gave us more time to train and motivate each other. I gave sales promotions and maintained a good office ambiance. As a business leader, you ensure that everyone, including staff and clients, is cared for with a great attitude. One negative person can hurt your whole team.

We tried to visit my parents in Mexico at the end of the year. Their visits to us became less frequent as they grew older. We always tried to include them in our hectic pace during that time of year. Sadly, I told Mom, "Sorry, Mom, we won't be able to visit this year."

She said, "Oh no, how sad, but I understand."

I shared Mom's sadness with my husband and asked if we could make a quick visit.

He replied, "Let me see."

Manuel always strives for my happiness. At the end of 2009, airline tickets were too expensive. Instead, he made sure our Honda Odyssey was reliable enough to drive the long trip. The following day, he happily agreed, "Let's go!" I called mom and told her we were coming. She got very excited. Manny was going to stay behind, work at the office, and be in charge. We took Stephanie, age 18, and Jordan, age 14, with us. They really enjoyed visiting their grandparents.

When we got to Mom's house, she had a tasty dinner all ready for us. She always made sure we were well-fed and happy. If we drove, we would stay for three weeks since we'd spend two days traveling. Once we arrived, we planned where to take them around the city. As always, our focus was on them. Everyone told us we spoiled them, but we didn't care about those comments.

Chapter Thirteen

BITTERSWEET

In March 2010 I won a Life Insurance recognition in Palm Springs, California. This time, no guests were included. Manuel volunteered to drive the 3 ½ hour trip. I invited Jordan to come with us. After we got there, Manny called to inform me that my mom was going to the hospital and requested that I call her. I had a strange feeling after I talked to her. She was healthy, and I had just seen her in December. After three days away, I couldn't wait to return home and speak with Mom. By this time, she had gone home after her surgery and was fine. Just a month later, I got a call stating that the doctor felt we should come be with her. Mom had her 10 siblings gather around her. We prayed together and had faith that she would be healed. No one knew exactly what was going on with her. I stayed in Mexico for over a week and then returned home to take care of my business. I was in denial of the situation. I called my friend, Dr. Mary Berretto for advice. If Mom passed away, what would I do?

Mary reminded me of the great cycle of life. After all, my mom was 82. I tried to accept the worst.

On May 12th at 5 a.m., my brother called me with the news that Mom had passed. My heart broke. I cried and cried like a baby. I took care of the most important matters at the office and planned on buying a plane ticket home. I couldn't accept the news and stayed in denial. I felt such guilt for leaving her and coming home. My mom needed me, and I just left her. What kind of daughter was I? I had claimed to love her more than anything, but I left her. I was a coward because I couldn't confront the truth. Deep in my heart, this was the truth that I felt.

Everything changed. I asked my husband if he would come with me. We bought emergency airline tickets for that day. We flew to Mexico with my siblings who lived nearby. As soon as we landed, we went directly to the funeral home. Fortunately, I had prepared by bringing extra money in case we needed it for her funeral, which proved helpful! We told Dad we would handle the expenses and divided the cost among all of us. I thanked God for blessing my business to assist with my mom's expenses. Before her emergency, I had received the honor of a promotion. However, instead of traveling to New Orleans, I traveled to Mexico to bury my mom. I called Farmers Marketing and told them I had to cancel everything. Of course, they empathized and understood.

After her death, I was so heartbroken I had to slow down a little. I took a couple of days off, but all I did was cry. I made up my mind to move forward and continue my life. It's difficult to do that with a broken heart. For a few months, my sales declined as I attempted to get back on track. My friends were there to cheer me up. They invited me to lunch and reminded me that Mom was my cheerleader in heaven. She was my angel now. I believed them. All the love and support I was receiving was terrific. I got closer to God. I felt my mom's presence when I prayed, especially in church. Thanks to her, I had faith in God. I knew God existed throughout all my adversities. I frequented Christian bookstores when I had time and found books to read that helped me heal. I sought therapy to overcome the intense guilt I had, which also helped me. A few months later, with my staff's help, our production and sales went back up. My staff was highly supportive, especially my son, Manny. My husband was an excellent supporter as well.

Now, my dad, an 88-year-old widow, had to live alone. My sister Carmen was nice enough to invite him to live in the United States. Dad accepted, but that only lasted a few months. He had the idea of being buried in Mexico with my mom, so he went back. Almost every day, Dad would visit Mom at the cemetery. They were married for about sixty-five years, an entire lifetime. With Dad permanently in Mexico, I asked Manuel to help prioritize his care. With tears in his eyes, he said, "I will help as if he were my dad."

I got emotional and said, "Wow, after Dad disapproved of our marriage, you forgave him?"

"Of course," he said, "I love him! I saw in your dad the father I did not get to enjoy due to my dad's alcoholism." Seeing my dad all alone now helped him and Manuel build a special bond. They became terrific friends. Manuel enjoyed Dad's conversations from his past. Because my husband had grown up with his grandfather, they had a perfect relationship.

We made it a point to visit Dad in Mexico as much as possible. Sometimes, we flew out to spend time with him four times a year. I learned about his doctors, nurses, housekeeper, and financial statements. We also took care of his house and ensured safe living conditions. I became involved in managing his money. Despite being in a different country, my experience as a Financial Services and Insurance Agent helped him trust me. He knew he could count on me, and I was so proud I could handle helping him. I felt exceptional. I had forgiven him for his negative ways as I was growing up. Now I could see what God had planned for me. As I faced challenges in building my business and getting my license, He readied me for managing my dad's money. I feel God chose me and Manuel for this beautiful journey.

I love looking back on my life and seeing how things have fallen into place. I've observed that there's always a reason and purpose behind every challenge. Nothing good or bad lasts forever. We kept our word. We started surprising my dad with our visits, and he got very excited once we arrived. Our visits were approximately ten days. I made sure he always felt special when we were there. I cooked his favorite meals just like Mom used to cook them. I started recording agency commercials for him, and he loved them! We also took a lot of selfies. We sure laughed a lot. Sometimes, I even gave him a haircut. He always looked forward to our visits.

Farmers Insurance held a Farmers Open at Torrey Pines Promo in 2011. Of course, I worked very hard with my staff to achieve the sales goals to qualify for this event. The company invited Manuel and me to join other top producers in San Diego/La Jolla, California for the Farmers Open. The professional P.G.A. golf tournament is held there every year on the last weekend of January. We got to meet Tiger Woods and other professional golf players. It was a beautiful experience! It's an annual event, and thankfully, we received multiple invitations because we met the sales numbers to attend.

Slowly, business returned to normal. Later that year, we received the honor of being invited to the Championship in San Francisco and Topper Club in San Diego. When we returned home from Toppers, we experienced something we would never forget. Stephanie told us she and her boyfriend were expecting a baby. We were astonished. At first, we were in shock, but later, we supported them the best we could, along with her boyfriend's parents. She had a healthy pregnancy. We planned a beautiful baby shower a month before the baby was born. We had an excellent turnout, and they received many things they needed for their new baby. We felt blessed.

Chapter Fourteen

INTERNAL FIRE

Our grandson was born in February 2012. He was a leap year baby! They named him Alejandro Jayden. It is a beautiful year to remember since we became grandparents. It was a big surprise from our only daughter, sweet and sour news. But love won! That baby taught us how our world was better with him in it. He filled a space in our hearts that we did not know was empty.

I wanted to spend more time with Jayden. I had to learn to delegate and trust my staff more. In the beginning, I found it complicated to step away. I was nervous about what my clients would say. Luckily, my son Manny had worked for me for eight years, and our clients trusted him. Once he revealed he was my son, they trusted him instantly. But at first, it wasn't easy for me.

I started picking Jayden up from school and we would stop for ice cream or go to the park. I could do things I wasn't able to do with my kids. I felt blessed that God was allowing these freedoms. My clients worked much closer with my staff. I felt relieved and no longer guilty for not helping my clients all day.

As a business owner, my responsibilities were hiring, training, and ensuring everyone completed their work. I trained them in time management and to be knowledgeable about our products. I kept track of the finances and accounting. I was handling legal and compliance responsibilities. Managing and marketing sales were my favorite things to do. I inspired and shared ideas with staff to be sure our customer service was always exemplary. Other tasks involved managing HR needs, supervising teams, overseeing daily operations, planning new initiatives, and resolving technology issues. All these tasks were routine for me, and I enjoyed them. I was always humbled to help my team grow.

Manny became increasingly involved. I mentored him daily and saw him excited and ready to work every day. He was always ready to hustle and never appeared tired. Manny learned to follow my advice and wisdom to achieve success. He envisioned that one day, he could handle our family legacy.

Due to our successful production, I was invited to join the President's Council of Agents again in 2012 with Manuel. We stayed at The Greenbrier, a world-class resort in West Virginia's majestic Allegheny Mountains. We lived the experience but never forgot where we came from.

Thankfully, Dad was strong and alert enough to live on his own. He refused to live with any of his children, and we respected that. Our conversations with Dad remained warm and friendly since Mom's passing. She was our go-to person for discussions. Now that she was gone, my dad opened up to us. Previously, he would go to her, and then she came to us to communicate. I learned many things from Mom and Dad's younger years, including when and where they met. They met at the same place my husband and I met, at the Jardin de Moroleón, Guanajuato. How cool is that? We always looked forward to our conversations with him. He told us that Mom was a talented singer and had even entered a singing contest that she almost won. I had no idea! I was stunned and wish she had told me about it. As always, Manuel was highly supportive of helping my dad; the days we spent with him were very special.

Dad was strong and healthy when he turned 90. We still loved to surprise him with our visits. I still cooked him his favorite meals. Despite his lack of support and strictness, I didn't hold grudges. Mom taught me to let go and let God handle things. I followed her teachings. Since Dad was part of Mom, we felt her presence when we visited him. It was their lifelong home, and briefly mine. We truly enjoyed every trip to see him and helped supervise his staff (from caregivers to nurses). We made it a tradition to take him on short trips near his home. Excitedly, I asked my dad where he wanted to visit as soon as we arrived.

His cheerful reply was always, "I want to go where you guys take me!"

The farthest we drove Dad was a couple of hours away. We would have a lot of fun in our old VW Bug, with shopping, lunch, the zoo, or ice cream. To keep him cheered up, we were willing to go anywhere. Time is precious. I always looked forward to helping him with kindness and special care.

Having Manny handle the office duties when we were gone was always a blessing and brought me peace of mind. Every day, I thanked God that Manny had fallen in love with his insurance career, just like I had. My agency was in the right hands, which meant I could enjoy my elderly dad while he was still with us. Manny never complained. He loved his grandfather and felt honored to help in this way.

In 2013, Manny's efforts as an agency producer were recognized with his first championship, adding to his numerous awards. I loved that he could join me for the awards ceremony in Chicago. Seeing him there was an exciting glimpse into his future. Chicago was new to us, and we were eager to explore. It was a beautiful experience for all of us. Back at the office, we quickly planned to return. I'm pleased to report that we followed through.

That same year, our daughter Stephanie's husband, Alex, asked if he could work for us. I interviewed him, and just as I told Manny on day one, we were not family at the office. He needed to be trained and licensed. I expected him to take this job seriously. Like Manny, Alex would work his way up in the business. He agreed, and we brought him on. Alex learned quickly, became licensed, and worked hard. He soon earned the respect of our clients. We loved him and he fit in well with our office culture. We were glad it had all worked out and now we had another family member we could depend on.

Our team grew again later that year, when our beautiful daughter, Stephanie, joined us. Again, I made sure she understood there was no "special family treatment." She enjoyed helping our customers. Clients would confuse her for me, and she loved that! It was fun but challenging to own a family business. Our respect in the community grew, and we became an "Elite Agency" for Farmers Insurance.

As the founder, I was an executive on-demand who solved our business leadership challenges with expertise and empathy. I established a legacy that would maintain the reputation and recognition of our family name, both within our organization and among our Farmers Insurance colleagues. Our staff as a family consisted of seven members. The beauty of our team was that I now had more time to share activities I loved doing. I navigated through family dynamics and provided a clear roadmap for a successful business to continue into a second generation. Mentoring my family members by succession to become business leaders was always rewarding. I left the business door open to everyone, especially all family members. New staff simply needed to be open for me to mentor them. Over time, we started developing a plan for when my husband and I could retire without any constraints.

I established our office culture based on work ethic. I promoted humility, respect, discipline, and professionalism. I strove to show by example how important it is to give to others. Being a mom, wife, daughter, and business leader filled my heart. Deep down, I felt satisfied with everything I accomplished after surpassing so many of life's challenges.

There was nothing that brought me more joy than being a leader in my career and enjoying my accomplishments with my family. I knew I had done things right, and they were just as I envisioned them.

When you discover your *WHY*, don't take it for granted! Don't allow others to cloud your vision with negative thoughts. Those types of people usually live a frustrated lifestyle and cannot stand the success of others. Stay away from them. If they are family and you can't stay away, then be strong, listen, and let go. Pray and have faith in God, and He will open doors for you—doors you could have never imagined. Find an excellent mentor and then hold on to them. But first, look at their lifestyle. Are they sincere and trustworthy? Do you want to be like them?

I consistently put my passion into practice by treating people how I want to be treated. Remember that people feel and see positive and genuine energy in you. My clients pointed that out to me many times. Hearing that always meant a great deal to me. A strategic mindset helped ensure I was always one step ahead. This trait is essential to all leaders. As a manager or executive, I needed to be frequently predictive, anticipatory, and prepared for all potential outcomes. By being proactive instead of reactive, I was able to respond effectively to various situations, such as a new competitor, changes within our team, growing concerns, or opportunities for advancement. I was proud to be an agile leader with a big heart. When you have that internal fire leading you, you can make wise decisions and not feel paralyzed by indecision. To change your family's generational cycle, you need to be open-minded and learn from everything and everyone around you.

I constantly reminded myself that the United States provides unlimited opportunities to be successful in any area of your life. How far you go is solely your choice. The support is there. Have confidence in yourself and work towards your goals by adopting a mindset focused on growth. Continue to strengthen your emotional intelligence along with your mental toughness. Strengthen your willpower. Focus daily on motivation. Nurture traits that are linked to high potential. Cultivate solid social support.

I'll always remember the day my dad accepted the opportunity to join the U.S.A. Bracero Program. He sacrificed for his family and left us in Mexico to pursue his dream of bringing us out of poverty. It was difficult for him. I know he suffered until the day he could have all his kids in America legally. That memory remained rooted in my heart. I wanted to show him his sacrifice was worth it. I'm glad he could witness my successful life story while he was still alive.

I learned to convert every negative thought or situation into a positive one. I became happier and a stronger human. I can now share positive stories and continue motivating and inspiring others. My place in the community continued to grow when I was invited to join multiple organizations, primarily non-profits. I am glad I always said yes. Recognizing the value of people's contributions led me to contribute to my community. I volunteered as much as I could. My husband was always behind me, my support. Manuel's always been there for me, supporting my thoughts and ideas; some worked, and others didn't. It's okay, at least we tried!

We learned ways to communicate better with a life filled with so many commitments. I haven't had a perfect marriage. Who has? Ultimately, we attempted to support each other's personal and professional growth. As parents, we were there for our kids as much as possible. Are we the perfect parents? Of course not. I'm sure we could always do better. Are our kids the perfect kids? Probably not. We love them unconditionally; that's what truly matters to us.

Manny was invited to join us and celebrate Championship 2014 in San Antonio, Texas at a beautiful resort. We experienced so much history and enjoyed delicious food. We got back home all fired up! Happiness consumed us.

We were also still traveling to visit my dad, who was now 93 and still healthy and strong. Dad had become my go-to person when I felt stressed out from working so much.

On one of our calls, I said cheerfully, "Good Morning!"

Full of excitement, his first question was, "When are you guys coming to see me?" I immediately put a trip on my calendar so we would be sure to make it happen. Talking to him sparked my day. He was my daily inspiration on my down days. Besides scheduling a trip to Mexico, I had a dream that Manuel and I would take a trip to Spain. I had heard so many stories from Manuel about his second-generation Spanish grandfather, who had loved his trips to Spain. We wanted to experience that for ourselves. In the fall, we spent ten days traveling from Madrid to Malaga, Seville, and Barcelona. It was another trip we will remember always.

Once our grandson turned two, Manuel and I took a day away from the office when my daughter had no childcare. I'm so glad we have been able to experience love as grandparents. I could not experience this because my grandparents lived in Mexico when we came to America. We appreciated the opportunity God gave us. There is nothing more wonderful than the love and guidance a grandparent can give a grandchild. We cherished the time with him that we couldn't have when our children were growing up.

Now that our work life had shifted, we continued to be intentional about living a balanced life. We established clear boundaries through various methods. We followed a good work routine by leaving work at the office, taking lunch breaks, prioritizing tasks, delegating work, and maintaining good communication. Also, we put everything in writing! That way, nothing and no one was left behind. We continued the healthy habit established when the kids were tiny of walking every day. It was a favorite ritual for us. Manuel and I joined forces for gym sessions years ago. It became our best therapy as a couple, ever.

Manny chose not to join us at Toppers that year. I happily asked what trip he would like to take to help meet our yearly sales goals. Being a soccer fan, he excitedly asked, "Can we go watch my favorite team play in Mexico City?"

Without thinking twice, I said, "YES!" We had a fantastic time. The soccer stadium was elaborate from food to games. It was a tremendous experience for all of us. I was thrilled to see Manny carrying on my work by sharing his experiences with clients.

I was so happy enjoying my 15th year as a business owner. Each day brought its usual mix of surprises, challenges, and fluctuations. We received an invitation to the Championship 2015—Achievement Award Leaders. Calgary, Canada, was the chosen location this time. Manny made it again as well, and he could bring a guest. Calgary is home to the International Film Festival and hosts "The Greatest Show on Earth" at the Calgary Stampede! We looked forward to it and experienced it all. The Farmers Insurance Marketing and Planning team always treated us like royalty. These rewarding trips were truly motivating. We always made many new friends, had fun, and learned new ideas to implement at the office.

Stephanie and Alex wanted to get married. We joyfully contributed to the planning. The event included a beautiful Catholic Mass, followed by a stunning party with business associates and family in attendance. Our business associates were like family to us; we always made them feel special for the kindness and support they had shown us.

I thought it would be a good idea to give our famous banana leaf tamales to our associates every Christmas. By this time, we served tamales for open house parties, special occasions, and at Christmas time. They continued to be a hit!

Everyone looked forward to our visits to their office. It was such a great feeling to give and not just receive.

Jordan's decision to join the Air Force in 2016 took us by surprise and made us nervous. After some reflection, we supported his decision. At 20 years old, he was prepared for the challenge. We were very proud of him. He was a unique, handsome young adult. We watched him strive every day to be a better human. He demonstrated discipline, good manners, ethics, and a strong belief in God. When he graduated, we flew out to Texas with him. We wanted him to witness our pride in his success and his ability to exceed all obstacles. The entire event was such an exciting and emotional experience. Our whole family was there to support him. I am so glad we made the time since everyone was always busy studying or working. This trip allowed us to have some exceptional moments together as a family.

We were delighted that Stephanie and Alex were expecting their second child; a second grandson. He was a handsome and healthy little boy named Nathan Jacob. How happy we all were to welcome a Christmas baby!

In 2017, I advised Manny to start volunteer work and engage with our community events and organizations like

NAHREPVC. He was excited and said, "I would love to! But who will take care of my customers while I'm gone?"

I told him, "Don't worry, they will be fine. We got it." Many years before I had volunteered for that same organization. Manny applied and was welcomed into the group. He was happy to learn from various professionals in our industry. This new opportunity provided a great deal of professional growth for him. I could see he loved it. Manny was the office manager and agency producer and was doing a fantastic job! I was always excited about any opportunity to mentor him. I reminded him that even the strongest and toughest people have days when they feel like giving up. The few who don't give up are the ones who become successful. Understanding your purpose is crucial. Remind yourself of it daily. Pivot and change tactics if you must. Get help, go for a walk, talk to someone...just don't quit. Never forget your purpose.

Our community didn't miss the fact that we made a positive impact both in the office and out. We volunteered and donated clothing, furniture, and other items. Our business always went above and beyond. This was very important to us. Avoid busy work that hinders your progress towards your goals. If you are going to get anywhere, you must learn to master your time and take control of your schedule. No matter what happens at home or with family, friends, and customers.

Near the end of 2017, Manuel received a call from his family in Mexico City that his elderly father had become very ill. With tears in his eyes, he asked me, "What do you think? It's the end of the year, and it's expensive to travel now."

Manuel never had been a big spender, and I quickly replied, "Money should be no issue now. Let me see about the airline tickets." I found a good package to include our hotel stay and air travel, and I booked it. We spent a week in and out of the hospital with his father. The doctors said he was doing better, so we went back home. However, just a week later, Manuel's sister called with the sad news that their father had passed. I was grateful that I had been quick to support Manuel by making the trip to be with his father. When you leave your country to pursue a better life, this very situation is one of the prices you pay.

Chapter Fifteen

WORKING SMARTER, NOT HARDER

I continued to take my job as a mentor and leader seriously. I always sought ways to stay educated, by motivating and inspiring myself first. This way, I could help others. I would purchase books and get ideas from other leaders as well. I still loved learning. To inspire others, you need a clear vision that provides a sense of purpose and direction. This helps others understand how their work contributes to the organization. You must lead by example by setting lofty goals and showing commitment, passion, and integrity. People are more likely to trust someone with high integrity and a great level of honesty. Instead of assuming you know what people want, have patience and ask.

We always tried to make our Sundays special. By then, only Jordan lived with us. He enjoyed going to Sunday Mass with us. Mom had inspired a spiritual journey when I was a young girl that was still in motion. I educated our kids the same way Mom educated me. Thankfully, it worked and continued to affect the next generation. After Mass, we would enjoy a delicious breakfast at the nearby Denny's, followed by a bit of shopping. We had to walk our food off!

Manuel and I were approaching 35 years of marriage. In March 2018, we boarded the MSC DIVINA Cruise for a 22-day excursion. From the LA airport, we flew to Miami. Our cruise included sites in New York, Kings Wharf, Ponta Delgada, Lisbon, Malaga, Valencia, and Marseille. It was a wonderful experience. On this cruise, we thanked God for guidance, protection, support, opportunities, and unwavering faith. We looked forward to continuing our incredible path with hope, optimism, and promise to share our blessings with others.

Both of us were anxious about being away from work for such an extended period. We entrusted everything to God and kept getting positive updates. In 2018, the economy was great, and we were all diligently working at the agency, focusing on sales, production, and goal achievement. We got invited to Disneyland as an Achievement Club for Toppers, Champions, and President Council members. Manny was also invited. Farmers Insurance was celebrating 90 years in business. How exciting! Disneyland was going to be closed to the public. Only the Top Agents, Executives, and their guests would enjoy the whole of Disneyland Park privately. We celebrated every time Manny could join us. He continued to make us so proud, and I continually acknowledged his loyalty.

What better way to celebrate another exceptional year than in Nashville? Nashville is famous for its role as the capital of Tennessee and its association with the country music "Grand Ole Opry" stage and radio show. Our Topper Club 2019 members invited Manuel and I to join them. Nashville was one place I fell in love with and hope to return someday.

I don't believe my business success was based on luck. It was my dynamic and positive energy to never lose focus. Also, I remained humble no matter what stage I was in. Life has its share of ups and downs; it can throw you a curve ball, even when you think you have everything figured out. It's not just you who has those feelings. Everyone must overcome their struggles, and nobody's life is perfect. Valuing challenges allows for personal growth and the ability to stay calm under pressure. The way you respond to adversity reveals your true character and the depth of your value system. One thing that helped me was creating a plan. I was not only always creating, but evaluating that plan. This helped me learn to prepare and sometimes to even prevent difficulties ahead of time.

I knew I was not alone on this quest. I could always call my district manager or colleagues. I could talk things through with Manuel or Manny. When I shared challenges with someone else, I felt more relaxed and less worried. I learned from others. I was open to new ideas and then modified them to my way of thinking. I learned how to feel my emotions, not stuff them down. I tried to stay within a positive and professional circle. I was intentional about sharing my problems when I needed help. Another motto for me is, "What you give is what you get." I manifest it daily. When considering things, I always took a wide perspective. Maintain the big picture and keep your dreams big when facing difficulties. I accomplished more with this mindset than I ever thought possible. I never allowed negativity, fear or small ideas to hinder me.

Keeping a positive attitude, even through adversity, can be challenging but it is possible. It is a skill that is learned; it is not automatic. It begins with awareness in the mind. You can stop having negative thoughts if you master acknowledging and letting them go. You may fail at this many times! Trying again is the key. When you fail at acknowledging and releasing something that doesn't serve you, don't give up. The next time something negative creeps up on you, try it again. Once you have practiced letting go enough times, it will become almost automatic. Never give up. I encountered and conquered various challenges throughout my life. Challenges like handling demanding clients, troubleshooting problems, dealing with marriage issues, and parenting struggles. I didn't shy away from seeking therapy to express my emotions and develop a strategy to deal with them.

I also learned how to work smarter, not harder. There are multiple approaches to doing a task. However, there is one ideal way to do it. You become an expert by repeatedly doing things ethically and intentionally. In simple terms, I learned to face and conquer life's challenges by being patient, persistent, and optimistic. Remembering my purpose helped me thrive no matter how difficult the problem was.

Chapter Sixteen

EVOLVING WORLD

My mom had a dream of visiting the Holy Land, but she passed away before she could make that trip. I was determined to do it in her honor. I mentioned this dream to a friend one day and she sent me some information. When I saw the cost, I hesitated and didn't take any action. Sometime later, I saw a flyer promoting Holy Land tours. I reached out to Father Marco at our church, and he sent me some information immediately. He also mentioned he was the tour guide! Excitedly, I told Manuel, "I think Mom wants us to go to the Holy Land!"

He said, "Why?"

"I wasn't even looking for this information, but here it is. Let's go!" I told him.

Manuel usually takes his time deciding, but this time he got excited and said, "OK!"

I liked the idea that we would travel with a big church group from our community. I felt less excited when I got a call that my dad, who was now 96, had fallen. He was in the hospital with an injured hip. I was immediately nervous and scared for my dad. I told Father Marcos that I felt I should fly to Mexico immediately. He calmly helped me realize that canceling this trip and going to Mexico would change nothing for my dad. Father Marcos recommended we stay with the group so everyone could pray for my dad together. He promised to name my father at the daily Masses. This was a rough start to our pilgrimage. I'm still curious about the timing of this.

After a 15-hour flight, we arrived in Rome for two days. We even visited with the Pope. Afterward, we departed as pilgrims to the Holy Land. It was a ten-day spiritual journey. Manuel and I renewed our wedding vows at Cana of Galilee. We spent time at the Mt. of Olives in Jerusalem, where Jesus ascended to heaven. We were both baptized in Rio Jordan and visited several other places mentioned in the Bible. Throughout it all, I felt my mom's presence with me.

My good friend and colleague Gabriela Reyna is a fellow insurance agent. Gabriela founded *EMBRACE,* an organization dedicated to inspiring, educating, and motivating other agents. I was proud to be a member.

Gabriela invited me to speak at their conference in Oak Brook, Illinois. It was a highlight experience to speak about the passions of my heart and inspire the agents in attendance. Manny, Manuel, and I experienced the beautiful city of Chicago together. It was a fantastic time.

On March 13, 2020, the President declared a national emergency because of the Novel Coronavirus disease outbreak.

California Governor Gavin Newsom issued a statewide stay-at-home order to slow the spread of COVID-19. He instructed residents to leave their homes only when necessary. Non-essential businesses were all shut down. As a leader, I needed to stay calm and adjust our policies by following the directions from Farmers Insurance. I also reached out to our county for our local guidelines. We faced new challenges to support both our staff and our customers' needs. I made sure our staff showed support and empathy toward our clients. We had a deep respect and understanding of what others were experiencing. Sometimes, it takes only one act of kindness to change a person's life. Being fully present for our clients who called with news of deaths and significant health issues was our top priority.

Stephanie and her husband Alex had their third baby during the pandemic. It was a very nervous time to have a baby but also very exciting. Thankfully, Nelito was born healthy and handsome in June.

By August, things were looking better. I wanted to do something for my birthday to share some joy with my clients and colleagues. So, with my staff's help, I organized a "drive-by" party. We received wholehearted support from everyone invited.

When Jordan left the Air Force, he returned to college. He was studying from home while working full-time as a Security Guard at the community's COVID-19 vaccination sites. We were proud of his focus and dedication to helping our community while attending school. He rose to the challenge of that time. His graduation from Ventura College was also a drive-by celebration.

Despite our busy family business, we always prioritized our children's needs. We had learned to be both firm and kind. Our children knew we were serious when we were firm, but always knew how loved they were. We wanted to be an example of strong parents. We felt responsible for raising mentally resilient children with purpose and empathy. We just wanted to raise wonderful humans, and I believe we succeeded!

We were thrilled to welcome our fourth grandchild early in 2022. This time, Manny and his wife Jasmine gifted us a healthy, beautiful little girl named Natalia Rubi. We celebrated her joining our family. A new little girl was such a great feeling. Now, there were four grandchildren to continue the Barsuto legacy. A few months later, we visited my dad, who was now 99. The news of a new baby thrilled him. Dad could no longer walk, but we had a great time with him and encouraged him to keep going. I enjoyed cooking for him and tried to keep things fun by acting goofy. He had a caregiver during the day and a nurse during the night. Dad looked weaker and was not eating like before. I made a doctor's appointment to address our concerns about his health. The doctor reassured us that Dad is doing well for his age.

A week after we returned home, my sister Teresa called me early in the morning with the heartbreaking news of Dad's passing from a heart attack. I feel that Dad had wanted to spend time with me before he said his forever goodbye. Even though he was almost 100 years old, as a daughter, you never want that last day to come. After my mom had passed, I learned that life is a cycle, and you must be prepared. Dad was tired and needed to rest in peace. Looking at my loss from that perspective helped me to accept his death.

Jordan announced excitedly one day, "Mom, I want to join the police academy, but not here in Oxnard. I researched and would like to join an academy in San Bernardino."

Surprised, I said, "Why there? That's too far! What are your plans?"

He was analytical and a good planner, so he already had it all figured out. How could we say no? We knew he would enjoy this career. His passion for helping others has always fulfilled him. We needed to support him to reach this dream of his. We helped him find a place to rent while in the academy. Jordan spoke with us often and had a lot to share. While he was still at the academy, one of his calls had a different tone. "Mom, I met a beautiful girl at Stater Brothers Market!"

"Oh," I replied. "Is she a good girl?"

"Yes, I think so," he said. "I gave her my phone number; let's see if she calls/or texts." The next thing we knew, they were dating. Jordan was happy to have someone to talk with being alone and far from home. In January, we all drove out for his graduation. I was one proud mom to see him looking so handsome in his uniform. Soon after, Jordan called to announce he was preparing to propose to Stephanie. Startled, I blurted out, "What? Are you sure? You don't think this is too soon?"

He said, "No, I'm 100% sure!"

Those two have a beautiful love story. Stephanie accepted Jordan's proposal in February. They knew they wanted to be together forever.

Chapter Seventeen

GOD IS GOOD

With each passing year, my agency continued to grow. The Basurto legacy grew ever stronger. We felt excitement for my family's success. Manuel and I daydreamed about retiring around the age of 60. After 38 years with Farmers Insurance, I wanted to prioritize family time and travel with Manuel. Manny was ready to take on the challenge of purchasing the agency. He had saved enough for the down payment. He also put a financial plan in place that was favorable for everyone. Retiring at 60 was a challenging choice. I had taken enough time to get my son ready. He had paid attention and done an excellent job polishing his entrepreneurship skills, and continued to improve them every day. We were so proud of him. I knew it would not be easy. Well, nothing that is valuable is! However, his positive energy helped him take over this significant responsibility. He was ready when I was—an important compromise.

Manuel and I had decided that our last official day as insurance agency owners would be January 31, 2023. It was a day I'll remember for the rest of my life. It was bittersweet, but I focused on the positive. With the help of my friend Norma, we planned a memorable retirement party. I couldn't have been happier or more fulfilled with my accomplishments. There were so many special people present. They all meant so much to me. It was a glorious celebration.

My first trip was to my hometown of Moroleón, Guanajuato, to process the changes in our lives. I wanted to celebrate by visiting my parents' grave and thanking them for immigrating our family. I wanted to let them know I truly appreciated it and did not take it for granted. My successful career improved many lives, just as my parents wanted for all their kids. I also wanted to spend a few days with my sisters. My dad was originally in my retirement plans, but God had a different idea. I'm sure he's happy for us in heaven, and he and Mom live on in my heart.

My next trip was with my husband to Cancun. Manny wanted to show gratification for the opportunity to continue our family legacy, by sponsoring this trip for us. Manuel and I enjoyed five full days of celebration. We had so much fun, thanks to our thoughtful and generous son!

A few months later, I started feeling depressed. I missed my clients, business associates, and my full life as an entrepreneur. The lack of productivity started getting to me. Manuel came up with an excellent idea. He proposed we take a trip to Mexico, and he would drive, just like in the old days. I eagerly agreed, saying, "Let's go for it!" We made it fun and spent three days on the road because he would only drive in the daylight. It was therapeutic for us both. After three weeks, we were refreshed and ready to continue our plans and projects. Jordan's wedding was scheduled for September 8, 2023. He and Stephanie planned a gorgeous wedding to be held on a cruise ship. A three-day cruise to Ensenada, Mexico with family and friends. What a beautiful way to celebrate.

Giving him away on their wedding day was bittersweet for us. He found his ideal woman. I knew the first time I met her she was the one for him. I was thrilled for him and their future ahead. I wished them both so much happiness in everything they did. It was especially emotional because he was our youngest child.

We are so grateful for our family. Without a doubt, they are the most significant wealth we could ever possess. We learned to treasure every moment. We made our family story one to be proud of, remembered with many smiles.

I successfully built a business despite dropping out of high school. It's a blessing to see my family share a love for entrepreneurship. I am so glad I accepted the challenges before me. I never shied away from bringing my family and staff along with me. Many members of the community respected my agency, and I respected them right back. It goes both ways. You give, you receive. I have seen how crucial it is to lead by example with a strong, unwavering work ethic.

I wasn't planning this legacy when I first started out. Day after day, our hard work yielded results. God wants us to work for our blessings, and He longs to share those blessings with others. It is why it fulfills my heart to share whenever I can.

This book is the celebration of my many triumphs and challenges along the journey called life.

As I get older, I have learned to observe my surroundings more and more. Sharing my wisdom makes me happy. God has been so good at guiding my path. I have tried to follow it with no questions asked. He has been there, holding my hand every step of the way. I genuinely hope that this book inspires others and shows what accomplishments are possible.

No, I do not possess a high school or college degree. I do possess the will and positivity to persevere and not allow anything to stop me from self-improvement and supporting my community, family, and friends (Hayes, Caleb T., and Bart L. Weathington).

I am incredibly thankful to Farmers Insurance for the following hard-earned awards: Eight President Councils, 16 Topper Clubs, 10 Championship, and many other recognitions.

I plan to continue enjoying my family while I am still healthy and robust. I also plan to continue volunteering, working out at 6:00 a.m., and traveling. God is good!

SOURCES

(Liaga-Linares, L. "A Demographic Portrait of the Mexican." Origin Population in Nebraska. https://core.ac.uk/download/232774664.pdf. Accessed 2014.)

Hayes, Caleb T., and Bart L. Weathington. "Optimism, stress, life satisfaction, and job burnout in restaurant managers." The Journal of psychology 141.6 (2007): 565-579.

About The Author

Alicia T. Basurto

With over 35 years in the insurance industry, Alicia Basurto is a retired insurance agency owner, having achieved remarkable success. Alice excelled in maintaining a thriving business, training staff, and delivering exceptional service to her clients. Beginning her career in 1985 as a receptionist, Alice's dedication and bilingual skills propelled her to top producer and office manager roles before opening her own agency in Oxnard, California, in 2002. Under her leadership, her agency became one of the most prominent policy writers for Farmers Insurance, earning numerous accolades, including Farmers Insurance National Rookie of the Year and Personal Lines National Agent of the Year.

Alicia's family played a crucial role in her business, with her husband and children working alongside her. Alice values family above all. Now retired, she spends quality time with her husband, children, and grandchildren, enjoying the legacy she built with hard work, commitment, and deep gratitude.

To connect with Alicia please email here at abasurto@myyahoo.com